Elvio Lunghi

Umbria

SCALA

CONTENTS

© Copyright 1991 SCALA Group S.p.A., Antella, Florence

All rights reserved

Translation: Max Waldron

Photographs: Archivio Fotografico SCALA Group (Falsini, Sarri, Grifoni), except: nos. 4, 9, 30, 40, 44, 52, 66, 69, 75, 100, 121, 129, 147, 151, 156, 157, 164, 165, 166, page 97/I, II, page 115/I, page 124/I (Antonio Nicolini, Milan); nos. 37, 55 (Alessio Giorgetti, Rome); no. 38 (Archivio Fotografico ILVA, Milan); nos. 41, 122, 163 (SEF, Turin); nos. 42, 43 (Dino Sperandio/ APT, Assisi); nos. 46, 49, 127, 152 (Pubbliaerfoto, Milan); no. 64 (Luigi Tazzari/Grazia Neri, Milan); page 80/I (Marcello Mencarini/Grazia Neri, Milan); nos. 119, 120 (Fondazione Palazzo Albizzini, Collezione Burri, Città di Castello); no. 87 (APT, Foligno); no. 112 (Sandro Bellu, Perugia)

Printed in Italy by: Lito Terrazzi, Cascine del Riccio (Florence), 2004

Cover: Assisi, Cathedral, detail

Back cover: Perugino: Martyrdom of Saint Sebastian, detail. Panicale, church of San Sebastiano

1. Perugino: Adoration of the Magi, detail. Città della Pieve, oratory of Santa Maria dei Bianchi

neighbouring and rival areas which traditionally gravitated towards other territories with longer histories and more lively cultures. And this despite the region's age-old subjection to the Papal States and the hegemonic pretensions of Perugia which was preferred to the papal Spoleto as the regional capital.

The tradition of the mystical Umbria, a land of saints, poets and painters also has recent origins. It did not yet exist when the young Goethe, during his jolting journey to Rome, disdainfully avoided the "enormous buttressing walls of the churches built one above the other like the Tower of Babel" in Assisi's basilica, to run instead to the main piazza to admire the Corinthian order of the Temple of Minerva, endlessly bemoaning the awful service in the town's inns. The first to discover the legend were a group of German painters nicknamed the 'Nazarenes' for their long blonde hair in page-boy cuts. They had settled in Rome in the early years of the nineteenth century to study the work of the Italian primitive painters. In the soft features of the Madonnas by Perugino and the young Raphael they recognized the prototype of a pure and emotional art, a prelude to a sacred art on the path to truth. This was contrasted by the Romantics with the lay spirit of Enlightenment and the neo-classical pagan flood.

The ingredients which help to make up the myth of Umbria are the mysticism in the art of Perugino and the "Umbrian school", St Francis, and the beauty of the landscape; all themes which were widespread among art critics north of the Alps before being taken up in the elegant drawing rooms of *fin de siècle* Perugia.

In the meantime the local men of learning, in the throes of active Risorgimento polemic, were reconstructing the gestures of Biordo Michelotti, of Erasmo da Narni, known as Gattamelata, and of a warrior-like and rebel Umbria. After the unification of Italy the railway arrived and the poet of the "New Italy", Giosuè Carducci, made his appearance in the Valle Umbra. To the image of the land of saints and warriors he added another adjective, that of "green" Umbria, destined to enjoy long life.

With the train came popular tourism. At the beginning of this century Assisi became the most prestigious destination for artists, poets and men of

2. Giotto: Preaching to the Birds. Assisi, Upper Church of San Francesco.

letters from all over the world. They were attracted by a very successful biography of St Francis by Paul Sabatier which appeared in 1893, in which the writer stressed the privileged link between the Franciscan spirit and the Umbrian landscape. Sabatier himself was to complain to a friend years later that: "When I see the ranks of English aesthetes and American snobs whom I attracted to Assisi, I almost regret having written a life of St Francis". Beyond the literary myth there remains the image of a land constructed by man's efforts: the ordered patchwork of fields separated by rows of poplars and the draining ditches, the terraces and embankments for the olive-trees, the stone houses clinging to the side of a hill or on a knoll protected by the ruins of a fort. It was in this hardworking landscape that St Francis walked through the fields singing: "Praise be to Thee, my Lord, with all Your creatures...".

3. *Countryside around Montefalco.*

4. *Montone, one of the many characteristic towns of the region.*

3

PHYSICAL GEOGRAPHY

Umbria covers an area of 8,456 sq km, equivalent to 2.8% of the total area of Italy. It is the only region in the Italian peninsula to be cut off from the sea, enclosed as it is between Tuscany, the Marches and Latium. The present-day administrative borders correspond only partly to any ancient historical reality and are the result of political choices made after the unification of Italy. The four papal wards of Perugia, Spoleto, Orvieto and Rieti were united, with the addition of the areas of Gubbio and Camerino, previously part of the Marches, and Perugia was named capital. Rieti and Sabina were made separate provinces in 1923 and annexed to Latium, while Camerino became part of

the province of Macerata in the Marches. Only in 1927 was the autonomous province of Terni created, following the town's industrial and demographic take-off.

The present regional border follows the Apennine watershed to the east, as far as the Sibillini Hills (the source of the Nera and the summit of Mount Vettore are in the Marches) where it turns sharply and runs between the Norcia plateau in Umbria and the Leonessa valley and Rieti plain in Latium. It continues towards the Tiber along the line of the ridge of hills above the valley of the Nera. From Otricoli the border runs north following the course of the Tiber and turns west at Baschi

4

to enclose Orvieto and environs and the slopes of the Volsini Hills. After following the shores of Lake Bolsena for a short distance the border runs north between Latium and Tuscany along the valley of the Chiani as far as the lakes of Chiusi and Montepulciano. Umbria embraces the whole of the Lake Trasimene basin and the upper valley of the Tiber almost as far as Sansepolcro which lies in Tuscany.

The region is mainly hilly, about 60%, with mountains making up around 30% and the rest consisting of plains. The sparsely-populated mountain areas are the middle range of the Apennines, with the summit of Mount Vettore (2476 m) on the Marches side of the Sibillini Hills. On the eastern side there is a series of Subapennine slopes: the isolated hills around Perugia and the Subasio hill near Assisi, the ridge of the Martani Hills dividing the mid-valley of the Tiber from the Valle Umbra, the Mount Peglia group and the Amerino-Narni ridge on the border with Latium. The hills are covered by thick woods but the age-old forests have disappeared following indiscriminate felling in the late nineteenth century to provide railway sleepers. There is a predominance of deciduous woods, with the trees rarely reaching great heights due to the intensive exploitation. The species vary according to altitude and the exposure of the land to sunlight.

The western slope of the Valle Umbra and the Gubbio area has a gentler and more rounded appearance, compared with the eastern side which is harsher and irregular, thus encouraging settlements and olive-growing; higher up stand the woods of oaks, elms and holm-oaks. In the valley bottoms between one chain and another are the rare areas of level land which cover just 10% of the total area. The valley of the Tiber runs the entire length of the region. At Torgiano it meets the Valle Umbra, the largest depression in the region. Between the ridge of the Apennines and the wide stretch of hills behind the Subasio are the plains of Gubbio and Gualdo Tadino. Further south, in the flood plain of the Nera river, lies the Terni basin.

The Umbrian river system centres around the Tiber which flows through Umbria for half of its course (210 km) and into which almost all the water courses in the region drain. In its initial stretch the river is mainly rain-fed and thus torrential in nature. Below its confluence with the Topino and Chiascio rivers its flow steadies with the arrival of the waters from the Valle Umbra. The Nestore and Chiani rivers on the western slope have a more markedly seasonal flow, with frequent summer droughts. The most important tributary is the Nera which has an abundant and regular flow throughout the year and receives the waters from the Rieti basin; the Velino river enters it via the dramatic Marmore waterfall (when the spectacle is not interrupted by the hydroelectric power stations). The Tiber has played an important role in the region's history, isolated as it is in the heart of central Italy, without large plains or an opening to the sea; it led Umbria to take on the characteristics of a frontier land, a crossroads between northern and southern Italy, between the Tyrrhenian and mid-Adriatic seas.

Within this frame, roughly in the shape of a heart, there live a little over 800,000 people (817,852 on 31 December 1986), distributed between 92 communes and two provinces, Perugia and Terni. In terms of population distribution, the province of Perugia prevails over that of Terni (72.3% against 27.7%) but its larger area means that the density is lower here (93 inhabitants per sq km compared with 107 in the province of Terni). The average over the whole region (97 per sq km) is considerably lower than the national average.

Umbria's population is becoming older. The crisis

in the share-cropping system in the years immediately after the Second World War was followed by a wave of migration, second only to the great flight from the countryside which took place between 1910 and 1914 when about a quarter of the population left Umbria. This has brought about a considerable reduction in the resident population and the depopulation of the mountain areas which were unable to meet the demand for work.

Conversely, in recent decades there has been a constant increase in population around the two provincial capitals and in the area around Foligno where the region's most important production activities are concentrated. Recent economic stagnation has averted the risk of an excessive concentration of the population in the towns and an uninterrupted process of urbanisation which would have upset the balance between town and country. This phenomenon has been displayed on a smaller scale in Perugia's northern suburbs and in Terni's post-war building developments. Elsewhere the population has moved down from the hills, attracted by the job opportunities offered by small family-run businesses which have spread out along the main roads.

5. The valley of the Vigi near Sellano.

6. View of Lake Trasimene.

7. The Colfiorito plain at the border with the Marches.

8. The Tiber in the vicinity of the Forello gorges.

6

7

8

5. *The valley of the Vigi near Sellano.*

6. *View of Lake Trasimene.*

7. *The Colfiorito plain at the border with the Marches.*

8. *The Tiber in the vicinity of the Forello gorges.*

6

7

8

UMBRORUM GENS ANTIQUISSIMA ITALIAE

Pliny tells of a tradition according to which the Italian peninsula was populated by the Umbrians after the Great Flood. The Umbrians were an Italic people of Indo-European roots, devoted mostly to stock-raising and tending towards nomadism. They established themselves in a huge territory on the peninsula's eastern side between the Piceno and Po river which includes the ridge of the central Apennines to the east of the Tiber. This area has been crossed since the earliest historical age by river and land communication routes and linked by mountain passes. The course of the river served as a line of demarcation with the neighbouring Etruscans from whom they differed in their use of the land, as well as by their language and foreign descent. The Etruscans maintained a closer relationship between town and country since their economy was mainly agricultural. The ancient Umbrians lived in scattered fortified settlements situated on the summits of hills. Contact with the urban civilization of Etruria, combined with the need to defend themselves from Roman attack, particularly after the opening of the Via Flaminia in

220 B.C., forced the Umbrians to group together in associations and to defend their settlements with large polygonal walls built with blocks of stone cut into irregular shapes. These Cyclopean walls are preserved at Amelia, Spoleto, Todi, Narni, Monte Sant'Erasmo near Cesi and Plestia near Colfiorito. The most important villages, however, were Otricoli, Camerino, Assisi and Gubbio.

The *Iguvine Tables*, containing the most important ritual text of the ancient world, were discovered at Gubbio. There is nothing similar either in Latin or Greek, and to find a parallel we must turn to works from the Near or Far East. The tables are seven bronze plates of various size, engraved at different times; the oldest date back to 200-120 B.C. and the most recent to 150-70 B.C. The common language is Umbrian while the characters are partly Etruscan and partly Roman. This use of two characters allowed the inscriptions to be deciphered, since the Latin text repeats the other but with more details. They were discovered in 1444 on the site of the Roman theatre and purchased in 1456 by the Gubbio Commune. The tables describe in detail

the religious ceremonies performed by the priestly brotherhood of the *Atiedii*. The most complex rite is the Expiation, the purification of the Fisia citadel and the town, on the basis of which scholars have sought to reconstruct the appearance of the primitive town. The beginning of the ceremony itself was preceded by the observation of birds by an augur who waited silently for a woodpecker and a crow to pass over the temple area. If the signs were favourable, the flamen donned his religious vestments and walked in procession to the three gates of the town, the Trebulana, Tessenaca and Veia gates, offering animals in sacrifice to invoke the protection of the gods.

The Lustration rite, the purification of the townspeople, was also preceded by the observation of the flight of birds. Once the auguries had been obtained, the holy fire was lit and the flamen had all

strangers leave the town. The inhabitants were divided into their military units or religious groups and walked in procession through the streets of the town following a circular route. This was repeated three times. Along the route sacrifices were made to the gods. On the third lap, the flamen released three heifers into the assembly; the animals were chased through the streets as far as the forum where they were sacrificed.

This festive chase has been identified as an ancient precursor of the Candle Race ('Corsa dei Ceri'), the tumultuous procession in honour of the town's patron saint, Ubaldo, which takes place in Gubbio in mid-May. It must be said that the inhabitants of Gubbio have a reputation for wildness and this mixture of the sacred and profane is no surprise.

The land to the west of the Tiber belonged to the Etruscans of Perugia and Orvieto. The contrast between the two civilizations can even be recognized in the landscape which is harsh and mountainous in the Umbrian area and gentle and hilly where the Etruscans lived. Perched on the summit of a hill, from which it dominated the valley of Spoleto and access to Lake Trasimene, Perugia is the furthest

9. *The imposing polygonal walls of Amelia.*

10, 11. *Two examples of the Iguvine Tables from the Museo Civico at Gubbio.*

12

inland of the twelve cities of the Etruscan League. Though situated far from the sea, Perugia flourished in the 4th century B.C. thanks to the large stretches of land planted with wheat, and the rich fish reserves in the lake. The power won by the town is demonstrated by its formidable walls, and the technological development of the local craftsmen by the quality of the bronze objects unearthed in the necropolises around the town.

Further south, atop a volcanic tufa outcrop at the confluence of the Tiber and Paglia rivers, stands Orvieto, the ancient *Volsinii*. It was the most important town in inland Etruria and one which exercised religious leadership, this being confirmed by the promotion of the *Fanum Voltumnae*, situated on its territory, to the status of Etruscan federal shrine. The town was governed by an extremely cultured class, who spent huge sums acquiring magnificent collections of grave goods of Attic pottery, and who encouraged local artists to follow the formal models of Greek civilization in the town's temples. When *Volsinii* was conquered by the Romans in 265 B.C. over 2000 bronze statues were discovered within its walls.

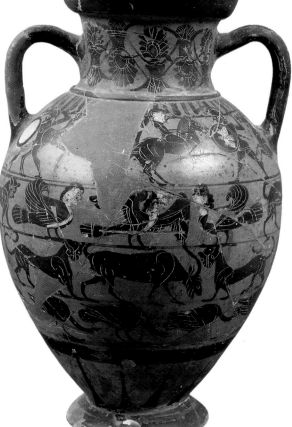

14

15

16

12. *The Volumni hypogeum, the great Etruscan tomb just out-side Perugia.*

13. *Etruscan bronze statue representing a warrior with a lance from the Museo Archeologico at Perugia.*

14. *The Mars of Todi, a bronze sculpture of the late 5th century BC, now in the Vatican Museums.*

15, 16. *Clay head of the 5th century BC and Corinthian-style amphora on display in the Museo Claudio Faina at Orvieto.*

ROMAN COLONIZATION

At the end of the 4th century the Romans began to penetrate the upper valley of the Tiber. Preceded by a series of military operations which saw the Umbrians and Etruscans allied in a desperate attempt to stem the advance of the Roman troops, the conquest was completed with the foundation of the Roman colonies of *Narnia* (Narni), *Spoletium* (Spoleto) and *Aesis* (Jesi) in present-day Umbria, and *Sena Gallica* (Senigallia) in the present-day Marches. This allowed the quaestor Caius Flaminius to lay, in Roman territory, the route linking up with the Adriatic in 220 B.C. The Via Flaminia crossed the border with Latium at Otricoli and passed through *Narnia, Carsulae, Mevania, Forum Flaminii* and *Nuceria* before crossing the Apennine mountains at Scheggia. Under the late Empire (3rd century A.D.) this stretch declined in favour of a side road which ran from Narni through Interamna and Spoletium and rejoined the original route in the valley of the Topino near *Forum Flaminii*, the present-day San Giovanni Profiamma. Once the area was pacified through supremacy of arms, the respect shown towards the ethnic and cultural make-up of the conquered peoples encouraged the Umbrian and Etruscan towns to declare their loyalty to Rome, receiving in exchange peaceful coexistence and favourable federative links, essential for the well-being and prosperity of the inhabitants. The nomadic economy based on stock-raising was gradually converted to an agricultural base. This was accompanied by the foundation of a series of towns on the flat land crossed by the Via Flaminia which increasingly replaced the valley of the Tiber as the source of trade and population growth. This, in turn, encouraged a cultural and economic harmony between the original Umbrian stock and the new Latin colonists who were united by religious beliefs of Indo-European origin. The level of integration of the two peoples was confirmed during the Second Punic War when the Umbrian towns refused to provide help to Hannibal's army which had triumphed over the Roman legions at the battle of Trasimene (217 B.C.).

Ethnic divisions were abolished by the *Lex Julia* of 90 B.C. which granted Roman citizenship to all Italic peoples and set up the municipium institution. This form of government took over the functions previously performed by the local communities, in accordance with directives from Rome. At the time of the civil struggles, the provincial land-owners sought in vain to oppose the expropriation of their land in favour of the veterans from Caesar's and Octavian's armies; this induced them to support the faction led by Mark Anthony. Memories of this are to be found in the poetry of Virgil, who came from Mantua, and Propertius, a native of Assisi. The war's epilogue took place in 41 B.C. in Perugia where Lucius Antonius, the brother of the triumvir Mark, had sought refuge. The starving town fell after a long seige laid by Octavian's troops. In his support for an administrative reorganization of Italy, Octavian was the first to use the term Umbria to describe the *Regio VI*, which included the territory to the east of the Tiber, in accordance with the ethnic border represented by the river. It stretched as far as the Adriatic coast between Pesaro and Fano, while all the land to the west of the Tiber was included in the *Regio VII* Etruria and Norcia in the *Regio IV Sannio*. The situation remained unchanged until the 4th century A.D. when Diocletian slightly altered the imperial arrangement by annexing part of the Umbrian territory to Tuscia.

Roman rule has left deep traces in the Umbrian landscape. The regulation of river flow and the draining of the marshy areas, particularly Lake Trasimene and the *Lacus Umber* fed by the Clitunno river, provided fertile land to feed the local and Roman workers. The ancient 'centuriation' appears again in the division of the land between Spello and Assisi or Gubbio. It was divided into regular plots to be awarded to war veterans, but reverted to marshland during the Middle Ages. Their Roman origins can still be identified in the regular street layout of towns situated on the plains (Terni, Spoleto, Città di Castello). Everywhere there are outstanding architectural remains of the monuments and buildings erected during the imperial age, whose preservation the Gothic emperor Theodoric took great pains to ensure in 493.

For example, Assisi's stepped structure, characteristic of hillside towns, is still based on the walls built in the 1st century B.C., while the heart of the medieval town coincides with the square in front of the Temple of Minerva, a religious building in the Hellenistic style built on terraces near the primitive Umbrian centre.

17. The Roman Porta Consolare at Spello; on the right a medieval tower known as "the olive-tree tower".

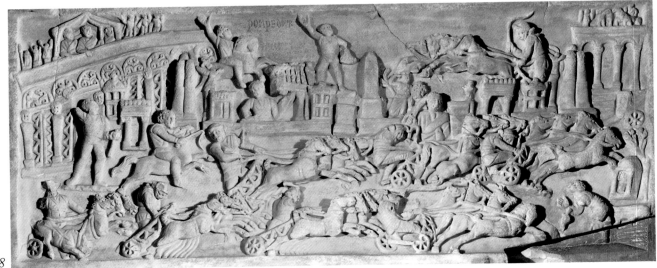

18

19

18, 19. Relief with scenes of the Circus Maximus and female portrait of the Roman period from the Museo Archeologico at Foligno.

With the advent of Christianity, the spreading of the new faith was helped by the Via Flaminia between Rome and Ravenna. Different faiths or cults passed along this road, and the *passiones* of numerous early martyrs relate that it was a favoured route for relics to be carried along. A severe obstacle for the spreading of Christianity was the strong link between the rural inhabitants and the pagan cults. In an imperial decree found at Spello (326 or 333 A.D.) Constantine authorized the Umbrians to hold the annual religious celebrations, gladiator games and the rites of the imperial cult in the town, while the Etruscans continued to gather in *Volsinii*.

Notwithstanding this, in the 4th century Umbria already had 22 episcopal sees, more or less corresponding to the region's most important towns. In the mountains between Spoleto and Norcia there settled communities of hermits and motley groups of monks in flight from the Middle Eastern regions of the Empire; they imported a contemplative way of life which inspired Benedict of Norcia, the founder of Western monasticism. The Sabine town preserves no traces of the canonised monk who spent much of his life in Rome, then moving to Subiaco and finally Montecassino; but his austere rule was adopted in the many *coenobia* protected by the solitude of the Sibillini and Catria hills or along the old route of the Via Flaminia through the Martani Hills.

20. *The Temple of Minerva at Assisi.*

FROM THE LONGOBARD DUCHY TO THE FREE CITIES

The barbarian invasions ruthlessly altered the Umbrian territory, destroying what the Romans had built. During the subsequent Goth war the Via Flaminia became the theatre of the Byzantine reconquest of Italy, which was completed in 552 with the Battle of Tadino when Narses triumphed over the Goth king Totila. The towns in the valleys were mercilessly sacked and destroyed and the inhabitants were forced to seek shelter in the hills. Important *municipia* such as *Scheggia, Forum Flaminii, Arna* and *Carsulae* were abandoned forever. Tadino, Trevi and Otricoli were rebuilt higher up. *Fulgineum* rose again around the tomb of Bishop Felicianus.

The Italic peoples had not had the chance to recover from the misfortunes of the war before another fearful invasion shook the entire Italian penisula. In their push towards the south, the Longobards established an outpost near Rome at Spoleto, founded by Duke Faroald I in 576. They

22

21. *Valuable evidence of Longobard art in the high altar of the Abbey of San Pietro in Valle.*

22. *The old apse of the Basilica of San Salvatore at Spoleto.*

23. *The Romanesque facade of the Church of San Pietro at Spoleto.*

23

controlled for some centuries a huge area between the Umbrian-Marchigian hilly region and the Adriatic coast. Longobard domination of the Via Flaminia interrupted the direct link between the Rome of the popes and the Byzantine Exarchate. Contact was maintained along the Via Amerina, protected by several fortified towns which had remained loyal to the Byzantines, Amelia, Narni, Todi, Bettona and Perugia, which the Longobards of Spoleto never managed to conquer. Thus the Tiber returned to being the border between two ethnic groups, or rather between the opposing interests of the Longobards and the Byzantines as manifested in the towns of Spoleto and Perugia. With the change in historical backdrop, the red thread of rivalry between the two towns wove the plot of the small struggles on either side of the Tiber which lasted until after the unification of Italy, and in some respects are still alive today.

During the Middle Ages the Italian road network was transformed, and with it the strategic role of the Umbrian valleys. Its stature as a holy city made Rome the destination of pilgrims from every corner of Europe who came to pay homage to the tombs of St Peter and St Paul. These pilgrims preferred the ease of the Via Cassia through Tuscany to the hardships of the Via Flaminia. The former route was to take on the name of Via Roma. Isolation, to a certain extent, favoured the duchy of Spoleto which was entrusted to an imperial vassal and survived the collapse of the Longobard empire after Charlemagne's victory. During the period of feudal anarchy following the dismemberment of the Carolingian empire Duke Guy III and his son Lambert (989-998) laid claim to the Kingdom of Italy and the imperial title. Only in 1198 did Pope Innocent III depose the last duke nominated by the emperor and replace him with a papal rector.

With the period of peace at the dawn of the second millenium the whole of Europe was clothed with white cathedrals, and a sharp increase in population discarded the static local economy and encouraged trade and the rebirth of the towns. The towns of Umbria, which had not been abandoned even during the darkest years of the early Middle Ages, united around the figures of the bishop saints, swarmed with building sites and began to organize themselves into a form of local power structures in the absence of any other authority. By 1139 Perugia already had its own consuls and undertook a programme of political expansion with its own army. The *comune civitatis* was registered in 1137 in Orvieto and in 1157 Pope Hadrian IV officially recognized the institutions of the free city.

Within the space of a few decades both the old episcopal sees and the country villas were freed from the control of Counts and in a short space of time the movement towards the institution of free cities spread throughout the region. The struggles between the pope and the emperor did not disturb the local governments which were intent on obtaining ever greater privileges by supporting one or other contender. The conflict between the Guelfs and Ghibellines was sharpened by the frequent visits of the popes to Orvieto, Perugia and Assisi, as well as by the presence of the Swabians in Italy. Foligno became a stronghold of the Ghibellines, while Perugia supported the Guelf cause.

The conflict between the rising merchant classes and the nobility, who (along with the monastic orders) held much of the land, took place against the background of widespread poverty alleviated only by public charity. It was in the midst of this society in turmoil, tormented by heretical movements, that Francis of Assisi (1181-1226) chose his way of life. His intense spirituality represents the greatest legacy bequeathed by Umbria to the whole world. Francis' decision to live as a Christian amongst the poor provoked a radical upsetting of people's consciences. Within a short space of time, the originally small brotherhood was transformed into a vigorous movement, the 'minor friars', whose self-appointed task was to pass on everywhere the message of Christian peace and fraternity.

The phenomenon was already powerful by the first decades of the 13th century, as the French cleric Jacques de Vitry, in Perugia in 1216 as a member of the papal court, was able to verify. When he arrived Innocent III was already dead but as yet unburied. During the night some thieves had stripped his corpse of all the precious objects and vestments, leaving his body almost naked and already decomposing in the church. At the sight of the butchery done to the corpse of the omnipotent pope, Jacques was deeply shocked, recognizing in it a sign of the ephemeral nature of temporal glory.

"I found, however, in those regions, a thing which was of great consolation to me: persons of both sexes, who, denuding themselves of all property in the name of Christ, abandoned the world. They were called minor friars, and minor sisters, and are held in great esteem by the pope and his cardinals.

These people do not concern themselves in the least with temporal things but rather, with fervent

24. *The Palazzo dei Consoli at Gubbio.*

25

25. *Giotto: Renunciation of Worldly Goods, detail. Assisi, Upper Church of San Francesco.*

desire and vehement effort, strive each day to tear from vain worldliness the souls who are about to drown and to take them into their ranks. And, through divine grace, they have already brought forth great fruits and many have benefited from them, so much so that those who listen to them invite the others: come and you shall see with your own eyes.

These people live according to the rules of the primitive Church of which it has been written: "The multitude of the faithful was a single heart and a single soul". During the day they enter the towns and villages, enthusiastically endeavouring to draw others to the Lord. When night falls they return to their hermitages or to some other solitary place to devote themselves to contemplation.

The women, on the other hand, stay together in homes not far from the towns and accept no donations, living instead by the work of their own hands. And no small thing is their sorrow and distress to see themselves honoured more than they would wish by clerks and lay people ...

We were able to meet the man who was the original founder and master of this Order, whom all the

others obey as they would their general superior: a simple and illiterate man, but beloved of God and men, by the name of Francis".

Such an austere system of ideals could not withstand for long the dizzy multiplication of associates, many of whom were already poor because of their social position and sought protection in the arms of the Church. The process of clericalization set under way by the Holy See in its struggle against the pauperist heresies also gradually eliminated the itinerant life of the poor friars. After the death of Francis, who died on the bare earth of the Porziuncola chapel on 3 October 1226, a magnificent Basilica was erected on the hill of Assisi. It was both the tomb of the saint and the *caput et mater* of a flourishing and respected religious order. The

26

26. *View of the Le Carceri hermitage at Assisi.*

Franciscans, by now present throughout Europe, were seized by building fever. In his home country the phenomenon was on the greatest scale: there was no place visited by the saint, no town where there was not a church or chapel consecrated in his name. The concurrent achievements of other mendicant orders (Dominicans, Servants of Mary, Augustinians, etc.) contributed in no small way to changing urban layouts, with the construction of monumental convents built close to the walls of the expanding towns. The more spiritual aspects of the Franciscan model also involved lay people. In 1260 Raniero Fasani established the Flagellants movement, made up of men and women gathered in confraternities who used to accompany their collective penitence with religious chants in vernacular Italian. The canticles or hymns found a great voice in the powerful poetry of Jacopone da Todi.

FROM THE PAPAL STATES TO THE UNIFICATION OF ITALY

During the 14th century in central and northern Italy we witness a crisis in the free cities, and the creation of family dynasties. Umbria did not remain unaffected by the phenomenon which was facilitated by the exile of the papal court to Provence and the loss of prestige by the rectors of the duchy when the see was transfered to Montefalco. This led to the formation of the earliest governments by the nobles: the Trincis in Foligno, the Gabriellis in Gubbio, Pietro Pianciani in Spoleto and the Monaldeschis in Orvieto. Perugia was the only city-state to retain for long its self-government by the people. During the popes' stay in Avignon, Perugia replaced papal authority in the region, extending its influence over the majority of towns in Umbria and some areas of Tuscany and the Marches. The return of the Holy See to Italy, vigorously encouraged by St Catherine of Siena, was preceded by the armies of Cardinal Albornoz. He conquered the land of the old duchy on behalf of the Church, had the forts at Assisi, Spoleto, Narni and Piediluco built to stifle at birth any revolt by the people, and forced the powerful Perugia to surrender. Even so, Cardinal Albornoz was unable to eradicate the power of the nobles which flourished throughout the following century without, however, giving rise to one dominant family. Braccio Fortebraccio da Montone (died 1424) and the Baglionis of Perugia, the Vitellis at Città di Castello, the Trincis at Foligno (until 1439), the Montefeltros in Gubbio (from 1385) and the Da Varanos at Camerino, surrounded themselves with men of letters and composers, constructed magnificent homes and led refined and luxurious lives, alternating with armed exercises, all of which made their courts thriving centres of the Renaissance.

27. *The courtyard of Palazzo Trinci at Foligno.*

28. *Pellegrino di Giovanni: Music. Palazzo Trinci, Room of the Liberal Arts and the Planets.*

29. *Ottaviano Nelli: Banishment of St Zacharias, detail of the courtiers. Palazzo Trinci, Chapel.*

During the same years Paoluccio Trinci rekindled the early Franciscan ideals, fleeing the comfortable convents in the towns to return to the woods, to the hermitages depopulated by the Black Death of 1348. Under the leadership of Bernardine of Siena, the friars of the strict Observants won innumerable followers who lived in small monasteries far from the bustle of the towns, and went into the squares to preach the renunciation of worldly goods.

This circulation of men and ideas was a particular stimulus to the figurative arts. "Between 1470 and 1490 Perugia was a vital point, more important in many respects than Florence. Perugia was the home of a movement which is an excellent illustration of the powerful effect stimulated, we believe, by Piero, by virtue of which the concept of art itself was carried to a higher level. Towards 1460 Perugia, to a much greater extent than Siena, saw a concentration of all the forms of graceful painting, all the models of that exquisite art which is expressed in architecture by the facade of the Oratory of San Bernardino by Agostino di Duccio (1457-1461). The painters Giovanni Boccati, Benedetto Bonfigli and Bartolomeo Caporali elaborated a sort of elegant assimilation of the chromatic taste of Fra Angelico, Domenico Veneziano and Benozzo Gozzoli. Their art was to age quickly; but was of such gentleness and elegance that something would remain in the works of the two greatest artists of the end of the century: Fiorenzo di Lorenzo and Pietro Vannucci, known as Perugino. These artists collaborated on the most important complex of paintings of this privileged moment: the delightful series of seven paintings on wood of the "Life of St Bernardine" (1473) in which imaginary architecture triumphs, as a rosy dream, in one of

30

the greatest creations of the Quattrocento. Two discoveries distracted Perugino from this delicious but minor style: that of the firm Florentine painting of the school of Verrocchio, and that of Piero's grand style. Perugino was soon to finish within the closed circle of a mannered and commercial style, while Fiorenzo confined himself within the limits of provincial specialization. Perugino nevertheless still represented such an elevated form of painting that the young Raphael was to come from Urbino to Perugia to collaborate with the famous master on the decoration of the Collegio del Cambio (1500)". (André Chastel, *Les villes de la Renaissance*).

This was a brief interlude which sadly ended with complete subjection to the Church. On 5 June 1540 Pier Luigi Farnese, son of Paul III and standard-bearer of the Holy Roman Church, overcame Perugia's final resistance. The town had rebelled against the pope because of the imposition of a tax on salt which was held to be unjust. When the city had been stripped of its statutory rights and the houses of the Baglionis demolished, Farnese erected a huge fortress, the Rocca Paolina, on the ruins. With its threatening bulk it oppressed the town for over three hundred years. Now that the memory of that servitude has faded, the people of Perugia pass hurriedly along the escalators which run through the heart of the fortress. Only the tourists stop to look at the ruins of the buried town where the houses of the powerful Braccio Baglioni were to be found, and know nothing of the reasons behind the saltless bread baked in Perugia's ovens.

The period of rule by the Church was certainly not among the liveliest when it came to economic advance and cultural development. The 17th and

18th centuries represented a hundred years of decay and widespread poverty for Perugia. Along with the beauty of the landscape, the plague of poverty frequently reappears in the writings of the rare travellers who braved the region's poor and inadequate roads on their journey towards Rome or Loreto. The entire social mechanism was centred on agricultural work. The land was in the hands of both the Church and members of the patrician class who practised crafts and professions but derived their noble titles from their possession of the land. The profits from the land were invested in the construction of town mansions, almost always made from medieval buildings which were enlarged and embellished to become the symbols of individual or family power. The share-cropping contract and the pacification of the countryside encouraged the building of large country villas and isolated farmhouses among the reclaimed fields which were inhabited by large groups of peasants. Small estates appeared in the hills and mountain areas as the people abandoned the defences of the walled towns and castles.

At the end of the 18th century the Napoleonic wars threw the territorial order of the Papal States into confusion. Umbria was divided into two departments, Trasimene with Perugia as its main town and Clitunno controlled from Spoleto. With the reorganization of the French empire in 1809 the two departments were unified with Spoleto as capital. The Napoleonic interlude brought with it great losses to the region's artistic patrimony. The Treaty

31

of Tolentino between Napoleon and Pius VI (1797) stipulated the repayment of the costs of the war in works of art and stripped the region's churches of the masterpieces by Perugino and Raphael which were sent to France to swell the collections of the Louvre. The revolutionary anti-clerical spirit drove monks and nuns from their monasteries and convents and marked the end of the charitable institutions, hospitals and confraternities, dispersing or destroying a wealth of possessions and works of

30. View of Narni with the fort of Cardinal Albornoz.

31. Sano di Pietro: Preaching of St Bernardine in Piazza San Francesco, detail. Siena Cathedral.

32. Giovanni Boccati: Madonna of the Pergola. Perugia, Galleria Nazionale dell'Umbria.

32

33. Perugino: Healing of Polyxena. Perugia, Galleria Nazionale dell'Umbria.

34. Interior of the Sala dell'Udienza del Cambio in Perugia, frescoed by Perugino.

35, 36. The "Agri" of Perugia and Spoleto in the 16th-century cartography of Ignazio Danti. Vatican, Gallery of the Maps.

art which had been built up over the centuries. With the Restoration only some of the stolen paintings were returned to the Papal States and entered the Vatican collections.

The French Revolution had the merit of spreading liberal ideas among the more enlightened members of the aristocracy and the new middle classes which had grown rich supplying the invading French army and purchasing the possessions torn from the Church. Perhaps the poor became even poorer, deprived as they were of the bread and soup distributed at the doors of religious houses, but Italy was made Italy also with the help of the Umbrian patriots. They flocked to the defence of the repub-

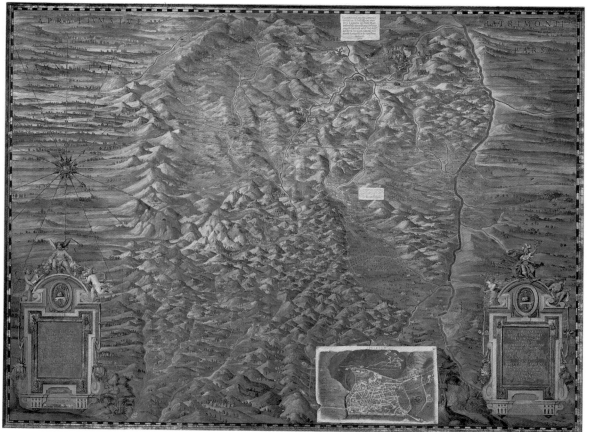

Museums and Galleries

To gain an idea of the variety of the Umbrian artistic patrimony one must visit numerous, municipal and diocesan museums. The region's collections were formed immediately after the unification of Italy with what remained in the churches after the pillaging by Napoleon's troops. To fulfil his dream of making the Louvre a universal museum of the arts, Napoleon had concentrated in Paris a vast number of works of art, handed over as war booty by the states which had been defeated in war. After the emperor's fall, the paintings taken from the churches in the Papal States (Latium, Umbria, the Marches and Emilia) were returned to Pius VI thanks to the good offices of the sculptor Antonio Canova, with the proviso that the works should be displayed for public enjoyment. From this time dates the inauguration of the Vatican galleries which still preserve the masterpieces of Umbrian art, above all the works executed by Raphael in Perugia. With the suppression of the ecclesi-

astical bodies in 1860 the old paintings remaining in the churches of monasteries and convents were confiscated as state property, so as to put a halt to the dispersal of these early works which were much in vogue among Romantic collectors. Unfortunately the collections thus formed do not represent a faithful mirror of the cultural role played by Umbrian art. So it is that 90% of the collections in the picture galleries of Assisi and Foligno, two towns boasting a great artistic tradition, consist in detached frescoes from roadside aedicules.

For works of classical antiquity the only institutions worthy of the name of museum are the Museo Archeologico in Perugia, displaying a large collection of Etruscan urns, and the Faina Collection in Orvieto, which preserves a varied collection of Attic black-figured vases. The most important of the local picture galleries (pinacoteca) is housed in the Palazzo dei Priori in Perugia and preserves paintings and sculptures

from the 13th to 17th century by local artists, with some masterpieces by Piero della Francesca and Pietro Perugino. The picture galleries in Città di Castello and Montefalco have recently been rearranged and the galleries themselves updated, allowing the paintings to be seen in their best light. It must be said that despite the fact that many of the collections are in a very poor state of preservation, the Umbrian regional government has set under way a thorough cataloguing of the local museums, and scholarly catalogues of the works are to be published. Assisi is a case in point, where all the museums are accompanied by catalogues and guides compiled by specialists.

Against this background of general mediocrity, some collections stand out for their exceptional interest, above all the Tesoro del Sacro Convento in Assisi. This museum displays the paintings and goldsmiths' works which once belonged to the church of San Francesco and the paintings donated by the art historian Frederick Mason Perkins. A small gem is to be found in the Museo Diocesano in Spoleto, which is being continually enriched with paintings and sculptures removed from the isolated churches in the hills so as to avoid the risk of theft.

I. Piero della Francesca: Polyptych of Sant'Antonio, detail of the Annunciation. Perugia, Galleria Nazionale dell'Umbria.

I

II. Niccolò di Liberatore, known as Alunno: standard of the Annunciation. Perugia, Galleria Nazionale dell'Umbria.

III. A room in the museum of the Opera del Duomo at Orvieto.

IV. Luca Signorelli: Martyrdom of St Sebastian, detail. Città di Castello, Pinacoteca Comunale.

V. Domenico Beccafumi: Adoration of the Child. Spoleto, Raccolta Diocesana.

lic of Rome in the 1848 uprising and made their own contribution in blood during the massacres in Perugia on 20 June 1859.

The arrival of the Piedmontese troops in September 1860 marked the end of the centuries-old domination by the Papal States. To recover the huge costs of the war the provisional government put both Church and the state-owned possessions up for sale. Their acquisition by the well-to-do classes further consolidated their large estates and worsened the already precarious economic situation of the peasants. The government transformed the large convents and monasteries in the towns into barracks, hospitals, schools and prisons, when it did not demolish them to make way for new piazzas. Museums and picture galleries were furnished with paintings and sculptures removed from the churches. The churches themselves were converted into artisan factories and workshops. The damage to the architectural and artistic patrimony of Umbria's towns was huge, with vast numbers of works of art, being offered for sale on the private antiques market.

The removal of customs barriers did nothing to encourage the Umbrian economy, which had inherited the backward agricultural policy of the Papal States along with the added aggravation of the collapse of the Roman market. Heavy industry came to Terni in 1875 with the opening of the arms factory; the town's favourable geographical position, far from the country's frontiers and from possible attack by enemy guns, recommended it in the eyes of the Ministry of War. The abundance of cheap water-based energy attracted the interest of capital from the north and earned Terni the nickname of the 'Italian Manchester' following the opening of the steelworks (1886), the carbide factory (1896) and the Italian linoleum company (1898). The call of the factory depopulated the mountains of peasants, but industrial Terni had been born.

37. Napoleone Verga: Festival day in Piazza Grimana. Perugia, Museo dell'Accademia di Belle Arti.

38. The Terni steel-works.

37

UMBRIA TODAY

On the threshold of the year 2000, the vision of the poor Umbrian peasant groaning and panting as he grips his plough drawn by pale oxen, in the shadow of the arches of the holy monastery of Assisi, is a rarity to be seen only on vintage postcards in a dusty album. The great exodus from the country in the early years of this century and the crisis in the share-cropping system immediately after the Second World War, which saw thousands of Umbrian emigrants forced to seek their fortune in Belgian mines or on the Argentinian pampas, has dotted the countryside with abandoned farmhouses and given the hill and mountain areas "a skeletal appearance. The slopes seem to have died, even if an occasional bush or grassy clod clings here and there. The tilling of the land which took place once upon a time has forced the woodland to retreat and today the crops have been replaced by tough vegetation" (H. Desplanques, *Campagnes ombriens*). This sense of desolation, amidst the silvery reflections of olive-

trees, the dark green of tobacco plants and the bright yellow of sunflowers, which have taken the place of wheat along the rivers, appears sad and romantic. The percentage of the population employed in agriculture dropped from 56.3% in 1951 to 11.2% in 1981. The collapse of agriculture has not been offset by a corresponding growth in light industry, and this has led to the desertion of whole areas, particularly in the hills. The population has concentrated increasingly in the areas of economic vitality: the Valle Umbra, from Perugia to Foligno and Spoleto, the upper valley of the Tiber around Città di Castello and the Terni basin, where there has been a proliferation of small and medium-sized businesses, often family-run, close to the road and rail routes. Now the emergency has passed, Umbria's agriculture is thriving, widely mechanized and devoted to profitable crops such as tobacco – Umbria stands in first place among the regions of Italy for the Virginia Bright quality – sunflowers

39

and horticultural products. There is widespread raising of pigs, cattle and other livestock (rabbits, pigeons and trout), though sheep-farming is currently in crisis. The hill areas provide excellent olive oil and good wine. The mountain areas are also enjoying a revival with the exploitation of woodland products (mushrooms, truffles, chestnuts and bilberries) and the spread of country holidays and hiking. Alongside agriculture an advanced food industry has grown up. The 'Baci Perugina' chocolates are famous throughout the world, but few know that Umbria is one of the largest producers of pasta in Italy and holds first place when it comes to the preparation of the highly-prized black truffle.

Alongside rural life, the heritage of the past is strongly felt in the crafts culture. A century after their foundation, the large chemical and mechanical industries in the area around Terni have not managed to integrate themselves into the region's economy and are slipping into a serious crisis of rejection. The figure of the traditional craftsman, on the other hand, is enjoying a strong revival, aided by the increase in mass tourism. As they work with iron or wood at the doors of their workshops they attract the curiosity of passing visitors walking down the quiet lanes and cobbled streets of the

medieval towns. The masterpieces of Renaissance ceramics are recreated in the Deruta and Gualdo Tadino factories and Etruscan bucchero pottery is imitated by the artisans of Gubbio. The blacksmiths of Gubbio and Assisi forge gates and tools for the home, drawing inspiration from the grilles and ironwork in the medieval churches. The coppersmiths in Orvieto shape a huge variety of objects. In Perugia stained-glass is made and cloth is woven on hand-looms. The women of Isola Maggiore produce Irish lace and pillow lace creations following a tradition introduced a century ago by the lady of the castle on the island. Fabric and table linen are embroidered in Assisi with the Franciscan stitch, a pretty variation of the cross-stitch.

Forced, every day, to come to terms with the burden of history and with a peasant tradition which constantly resurfaces despite employment in factories or public bodies (the cultivation of small plots of land as a secondary occupation is very widespread), the inhabitants of Umbria are conservative by nature. This traditional spirit explodes on hot summer evenings, in the commotion of the simple peasant festivities which sprout like mushrooms in all the country towns. During the year a whole

40

39. Rocca di Postignano in the Vigi valley, an ancient fortified town ruled by the Trinci family, now deserted.

40. The tobacco harvest.

41. Traditional hand decoration of pottery in a workshop at Sigillo, a small town on the slopes of Mount Cucco.

41

42

series of folkloric and religious festivals, inherited from primitive pagan society or the Christian Middle Ages, from 17th-century Baroque society or the peasant world, are held throughout the region. Impeccable in their faithful historical reconstruction, the most celebrated festivals include the 'Calendimaggio' in Assisi, the 'Corsa all'Anello' in Narni, the 'Palio dei Terzieri' in Città della Pieve, the 'Corsa dei Ceri' in Gubbio, the 'Giostra della Quintana' in Foligno and the 'Cantamaggio' in Terni.

Nevertheless, despite its marginal position, the region can also offer the visitor first-class artistic and cultural events: theatre-lovers can immerse themselves in the elegant atmosphere of the 'Festival dei Due Mondi' in Spoleto or the Todi Festival and enthusiasts of classical music will enjoy the

music rising from the theatres and piazzas of Perugia, Città di Castello, Acquasparta and Assisi. But perhaps what endears Umbria to the world is its vocation as a land of peace, beyond racial and religious differences. The salutation of "peace and goodness" was offered to the world by St Francis and taken up by Aldo Capitini, the philosopher of non-violence, during the March for Peace from Perugia to Assisi, in which thousands of people take part each year, eager to demonstrate to the world their hope in a better future.

ITINERARIES

Perugia and the Trasimene basin, the valley of Spoleto with its historic towns, the rural communities in the upper and mid-valley of the Tiber, the mountain ridges around Gubbio, the sun-drenched valley of Terni, the pretty course of the Nera river, the tufa plateau around Orvieto: these are the natural features through which the traveller passes as he crosses the region. After visiting the shrines in Assisi, anyone who wants to undertake a spiritual pilgrimage far from the towns, in search of the more intimate Umbria in the footsteps of St Francis, can go in search of the many silvan hermitages linked to the saint's memory: the Carceri, the Speco di Sant'Urbano, Farneto, the Isola Maggiore, the hermitage of Buonriposo, Monteluco, La Verna, Greccio. No less suggestive is a visit to the isolated Benedictine monasteries in the Martani Hills and the Catria massif. Hikers will find a wealth of well-marked itineraries of great natural interest on the slopes of the Apennines.

"Umbria is structured a little like the ancient game of goose: a compulsory route made up of a series of squares, in some of them the player pauses and in some of them he goes back. If the tour begins from Lake Trasimene or from Orvieto then part of the route is missing, but if we come from the direction of Rome then the stops are: Narni, Terni, Spoleto, Foligno, Trevi, Spello, Assisi... where it is a pleasure to linger for a while, where there is always something to see or eat or drink." (Cesare Brandi, 1975).

For those travelling with their own vehicle, the region offers a network of fast two-way highways centered on two main axes: the ss. 3 bis, or 'Tiberina', which runs along the valley of the Tiber from Sansepolcro at the border with Tuscany and Emilia Romagna, as far as Orte in Latium, and the ss. 75 bis, or 'Trasimeno', from the Valdichiana motorway link as far as Perugia, continuing along the ss. 75, the 'Centrale Umbra' as far as Foligno. The 'Autostrada del Sole' enters the region near Chiusi in Tuscany, passes by Fabro, Orvieto and Attigliano and leaves it again at Orte in Latium. The 'Flaminia', s. 3, is a fairly busy road linking Latium to the Marches, passing through Terni, Spoleto, Foligno, Gualdo Tadino and Cagli. The provincial and local roads are generally well-maintained and there are few unpaved sections except in the depths of the countryside and in the mountains. Rail connections, however, cannot be said to be equally efficient. The Rome-Florence line runs along the south-western edge of Umbria, passing through Orvieto. A regional line runs from Terentola to Perugia and Foligno. A more important role is played by the Rome-Ancona line which enters Umbria at Orte and passes through Terni, Spoleto, Foligno, Gualdo Tadino and Fabriano. The valley of the Tiber is served by a branch line running from Sansepolcro to Terni. Umbria has two passenger airports, Sant'Egidio at Perugia and Sant'Eraclio at Foligno. There are daily flights from Sant'Egidio to Milan.

Under Roman rule Umbria acted for centuries as a link between the Tyrrhenian Sea and the Adriatic, between Romagna and Rome. During the Middle Ages it was, above all, a group of towns, often in conflict, each with its own territory and its own area of outward expansion: Perugia and Lake Trasimene towards Tuscany, Città di Castello towards the upper valley of the Tiber and Arezzo, Gubbio towards Montefeltro, Spoleto towards Abruzzi and the Kingdom of Naples, Terni towards Latium and Orvieto towards *Tuscia*. In choosing the itineraries we have favoured the historical routes towards the bordering regions.

44. *The Abbey of San Severo and San Martirio in the Orvietan countryside.*

PERUGIA AND LAKE TRASIMENE

The gateway to Umbria from the Tuscan border is in the Val di Chiana near Cortona. In ancient times the Chiani river flowed towards the Tiber through a gently sloping valley, giving rise to troublesome swamps.

In 17 B.C., in order to eliminate the malaria-infested environment and to exploit the fertility of the land, the Romans conceived of a plan to divert its waters into the river Arno, thus reducing the risk of floods in Rome. The plan was never carried out and with the population crisis in the early Middle Ages the valley floor became gradually marshier, giving rise to the lake of Chiusi and forcing the few settlements to seek refuge on the hill-tops. In 1502 Leonardo da Vinci, a guest of Giampaolo Baglioni at Castiglion del Lago, attempted to drain the valley. He drew up a map of the area and proposed the construction of a series of drainage canals to control the flow of the stagnant waters, so as to link the Arno and the Tiber via Lake Trasimene and to allow inland navigation between Florence and Rome. This project was also abandoned and only at the end of the 18th century was agreement reached between the Papal States and the Grand Duchy of Tuscany to reverse the course of the river by creating an artificial watershed near Chiusi.

Once past Cortona, the low hills on the left draw back to create a majestic natural amphitheatre covered with olive groves and woods. In the middle of the basin is Lake Trasimene, the largest lake in central and southern Italy (it covers an area of 128 sq km) though it reaches a depth of only 6 metres. Lake Trasimene is a closed lake without any natural outflow and is fed only by rainwater: this explains its very variable water-level. For this reason, in the 19th century it was several times proposed that the lake be drained to produce fertile farm land, as had been done with Lake Fucino in Abruzzi. The Civil Engineers of Perugia, with the support of the local people, made an attempt in 1882 but the plan went no further than a reclamation scheme. The lake's appearance before the 19th-century reclamation project can be reconstructed thanks to a painting by Fra Angelico now in the Museo Diocesano in Cortona: the episode of the *Visitation* takes place against the background of the Val di Chiana, with the lake surrounded by turreted castles.

The valley feeding the lake covers an area slightly larger than twice the size of the lake itself, but the whole area is intensively cultivated. Thick groves of reeds (used for matting) have been planted along the water line; this has helped to protect the shores of the lake from speculative building development. The mild climate and attractive countryside, as well as the proximity of the historic towns of Umbria and Tuscany, have favoured the development of summer tourism, which in the last few decades has taken over from the less profitable fishing activities. Along the shores of the lake well-equipped tourist facilities have developed, able to welcome the growing number of visitors, above all from northern Europe, who are attracted here by the area's beauty and peacefulness.

Though there is no river feeding the lake, the water is clean. For centuries Perugia, protective of its borders, discouraged the growth of any large town on Lake Trasimene, hardly tolerating even the poor fishing villages built around the castles of Passignano, Monte del Lago, Tuoro, Montemolino and Castiglion del Lago which belonged to noble families of Perugia. The best-preserved of these castles is *Castiglion del Lago*, which was seized from the Baglionis by Pope Julius III and enfeoffed to his sister Giacoma del Monte, the wife of Francesco Della Corgna. He built a residence and had it decorated by Mannerist painters with the deeds of Ascanio della Corgna, who had fought at the Battle of Lepanto alongside the Christian forces. The town hosts an attractive kite and balloon show with participants from all over Europe, once every two years in April. The plain at Tuoro is famous as the site of the violent battle fought in 217 B.C. between the Carthaginians led by Hannibal and the Roman troops under Caius Flaminius, in which around 16,000 Romans lost their lives. Next to the small port, an open-air sculpture museum, the 'Campo del Sole', has been set up by the Sicilian artist Salvatore Cascella.

The three islands in the lake are linked by a regular boat service. The Isle of Polvese was recently purchased by the provincial government of Perugia and is used as a summer holiday resort for children. Greater attention is due to *Isola Maggiore*, a tranquil oasis of greenery with a pretty fishing village. St Francis stayed on the island during Lent in 1211 and the chapel where the saint lived during his stay can still be seen. St Bernardino of Siena and Pope Pius II of the Piccolomini family stayed in the Franciscan convent of San Girolamo, now converted into a private home. The church of San

45. *Fra Angelico: Visitation, detail of Lake Trasimene. Cortona, Museo Diocesano.*

46. *Aerial view of Castiglione del Lago.*

45

46

47

Michele is also worth a visit, for its frescoes by a follower of Benozzo Gozzoli from Foligno (c. 1460) and a *Crucifixion* by Bartolomeo Caporali. The inns and restaurants in the lakeside towns offer excellent freshwater fish: carp, tench, pike and eel. Roach, once the favourite fish among the locals, disappeared from the lake some years ago.

From the top of the hills to the south, the lake is overlooked by the castles of Paciano and Panicale. Further away, opposite Chiusi and Cetona, the red-coloured *Città della Pieve* stands on a hill-top. The warm-coloured bricks used to build all the houses and churches in the town gives it the appearance of a Tuscan village. Città della Pieve was the birthplace of Pietro Vannucci, known as Perugino, who left a masterpiece in the *Nativity* in the church of Santa Maria dei Bianchi. This alone is enough to recommend the town to visitors.

The hill of Monte Melino separates the lake basin from the Pian di Carpine; for centuries this was the name given to the valley carved by the Caina torrent, which was once covered by thick woods of hornbeams.

The valley was crossed by a pilgrimage route towards Rome. To welcome travellers the Hospitaliers of St John built a hostel here known as the Magione, beside which the present-day castle was built (c. 1420).

Here, in 1502, some squires of the Marches and Umbria plotted against Cesare Borgia, the son of Pope Alexander VI. In revenge these local lords were treacherously drawn into the forts at Senigallia and Città della Pieve where they were massacred. The Franciscan Giovanni del Pian di Carpine, author of the chronicle of his journey to the court of the Great Khan of the Mongols (1245-47), which was used by Marco Polo in the writing of his *Travels*, was born at Magione. The valley of the Caina is dominated by the castle of *Corciano*, a picturesque medieval walled town. The parish church preserves a painting by Perugino. During the summer the town's quiet streets bustle with the 'Agosto Corcianese', a festival of theatre and the figurative arts.

The opening of an important road in the valley has been accompanied over the last few decades by a considerable increase in craft activities, industry and commerce, causing serious damage to the ancient rural aspect of the area. Rural Umbria is still intact in the nearby valley of the Nestore, dotted with country houses and small castles. The castle of Fontignano, where Perugino died in 1521 and which preserves some frescoes by the master, is worth a visit.

Perugia stands on the top of a hill, protected by sturdy Etruscan walls. In the Middle Ages the town became one of the most important free cities in central Italy, the third most powerful after Florence and Siena.

Between the 12th and 13th centuries the

47. *The Rocca di Passignano on Lake Trasimene.*

48. *In the fishing village of Isola Maggiore.*

49. *Città della Pieve.*

48

49

50. Perugino: Adoration of the Magi. Città della Pieve, Oratory of Santa Maria dei Bianchi.

51. Benedetto Bonfigli: Madonna of the Misericordia, detail of Perugia. Perugia, Convent of San Francesco al Prato.

52. The Via Appia in the heart of Perugia; in the foreground the medieval aqueduct which fed the Fontana Maggiore.

50

"boroughs spread out over the hills, not unlike the fingers of a hand" (Leon Battista Alberti, *De Re Aedificatoria*), expanding beyond the Etruscan walls and pushing outwards from the town along the lines of the royal roads. Monumental churches and convents were founded near the town gates and encouraged its growth.

The power of the medieval commune was suddenly transformed in 1540 by the loss of its institutional freedoms and its annexation to the Papal States (the Salt War). During the following centuries the only modifications to the town's layout involved the patrician mansions whose facades and interiors were renewed by the local nobility, the owners of a considerable part of the earnings derived from the land.

The Etruscan town centre corresponds to what is now Piazza IV Novembre, at the intersection of the 'cardo' (the road in a Roman camp running north to south) and the 'decumanus' (the road running east to west), the present-day Via Rocchi and Via dei Priori. The piazza's current appearance dates from the end of the 13th century when the seats of religious and political power were built. The most ancient monument is the magnificent Fontana Maggiore, the greatest masterpiece of medieval

statuary, created by the workshop of Nicola and Giovanni Pisano (1278). The fountain was built to celebrate the completion of an aqueduct that would quench the thirst of the townspeople. In the square stands the cathedral of San Lorenzo, built in the Gothic style between 1345 and 1490 on the site of a smaller church. Opposite is the Palazzo dei Priori, one of the most magnificent civic buildings in the Gothic style. The Sala dei Notari on the ground floor preserves a rare example of painted decoration on a political subject (1299). Around this large room another block was built between 1320 and 1350 which occupied all the space as far as Via dei Priori and encompassed the towers of the Romanesque Palazzo del Capitano. The upper floors of the palazzo houses the Galleria Nazionale dell'Umbria, the most important art collection in the region. From one side of Piazza IV Novembre runs Corso Vannucci, the town's meeting place where the most elegant bars and shops are to be found. The Sala dell'Udienza del Cambio is decorated with celebrated frescoes by Pietro Perugino (1498-1500). At the end of the street is the entrance to the Rocca Paolina, a fortress commissioned by Paul III Farnese to punish the town for its revolt against the Pope's orders to pay a tax imposed on

51

52

53

54

55

57

53. *Piazza IV Novembre with the Palazzo dei Priori and the Fontana Maggiore, Perugia.*

54. *The Fontana Maggiore against the background of the Gothic Cathedral of San Lorenzo.*

55. *Giuseppe Rossi: the Rocca Paolina. Perugia, Galleria Nazionale dell'Umbria.*

56. *The Porta Marzia (2nd-1st century BC), which Antonio Sangallo the Younger incorporated into the walls of the Rocca Paolina in Perugia.*

57. *The Arco di Augusto opening into Piazza Fortebraccio in Perugia.*

The Roaches of Sant'Ercolano

In his collection of three hundred tales, Franco Sacchetti tells of a roguish trick played on the inhabitants of Perugia by Bonamico Buffalmacco, the jesting painter who appears in several tales from the *Decameron*: irritated by annoying entreaties to complete a painting of Sant'Ercolano, Buffalmacco depicted the venerated patron saint of Perugia with a crown on his head made of roaches, the succulent fish from the lake which are so appreciated on Umbria's tables.

The saying about the 'roach-eating people of Perugia' is not the fruit of the wicked imagination of Sacchetti. It is clearly announced by the sculptures on the Fontana Maggiore which were intended as a sort of encyclopaedic summary of medieval political credo and moral beliefs, imparted to the citizens by their government. The patron saint Ercolano appears here beside a

Domina laci, a Lady of the Lake in the person of a young maiden carrying fish – the roach.

The fountain was commissioned in 1227 in fitting celebration of an old dream of the people of Perugia: the construction of an aqueduct to bring running water up to the top of the hill on which the town stands; until then the inhabitants had had to quench their thirst with the water from Etruscan tanks. The design of the fountain was entrusted to the architect Fra Bevignate. The plumbing work was directed by the Venetian, Fra Boninsegna. The sculptural decoration was commissioned to Nicola and Giovanni Pisano, who completed the work in less than a year. At that time the podestà was Matteo da Correggio, and the capitano del popolo Ermanno da Sassoferrato, and both are seen in the upper circle assisting Eulistes, Ulysses' mythical companion who wrote Perugia's laws. The names of the fountain's creators appear in a long dedicatory inscription.

IV

V

"Observe, you who pass, the gay life [of this fountain.
If you look well you will see wonder-[ful things.
Oh Sant'Ercolano, oh Lawrence, [cease not to implore
Him who sits above the heavenly bodies to keep the waters flowing.
And may the lake and the rights of [Chiusi remain close to your heart.
Town of Perugia, be joyous and hold [as your father
The good Fra Bevignate who turns his hand and genius to every skilled task.
He is the builder of this work, he [directed all
And he must be praised with the sweet name Benedetto.
Able to bring order to things, he has [gladly given us this his creation.
These are the names of the excellent [sculptors of this fountain.
Nicola, famous in art, the creator of [ever pleasant works.
The most eminent of sculptors, he is most welcome among the ranks of [the good.
The first is the father, and his dear [son the other.
Who, if you will not be mistaken, you [will call Giovanni.
Pisans by birth and Pisani by name; [may they long live healthy.

Let it be known that the clear genius [which led the waters here.
Is known by the well-wishing name of [Boninsegna.
He executed the work and made all [the conduits and pipes.
Born in Venice he was, and beloved [of Perugia he is.
The fountain was completed in the [year one thousand two hundred.
To which you will add seventy eight.
At that time reigned as pope Nicholas III And Rudolph the [Great was Emperor."

I, II. Two statuettes from the upper basin of the Fontana Maggiore, representing the patron saint Ercolano and a 'Domina Laci'.

III, IV, V. Nicola and Giovanni Pisano: bas-reliefs from the Fontana Maggiore representing the months of December, October and November.

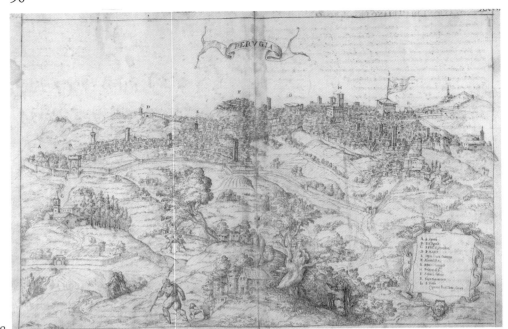

58. *Cipriano Piccolpasso,
Le piante e i ritratti...,
view of the city of Peru-
gia. Perugia, Biblioteca
Augusta, ms. 3064.*

58

59

59. *Raphael: The Trinity and saints, a fresco in the Church
of San Severo in Perugia.*

60. *The interior of the early Christian Church of Sant'Angelo in Perugia.*

60

salt. It is for this reason that the bread baked by Perugia's bakers is saltless. This hated fortress, the symbol of papal rule, was razed to the ground by the crowd which gathered on the arrival of the Piedmontese troops in 1860, and in its place the Palazzo della Provincia was built. What remains of the houses of the Baglioni family, which dominated the scene during the 15th century, can still be seen beneath the building; their palaces were demolished to make way for the castle. The streets of this subterranean Perugia are today linked by escalators, while the storerooms of the fortress regularly house art exhibitions.

The historic town centre has a typically medieval appearance. The winding streets following the contours of the hill are linked by steep flights of steps, often interrupted by the tall Etruscan wall. There are many historic buildings to visit: the oratory of San Severo, with a fresco by Raphael; the monumental church of San Domenico (1304-1458) and the adjacent Museo Archeologico dell'Umbria; the Romanesque basilica of San Pietro, one of the most beautiful in the town; the Renaissance oratory of San Bernardino, with its facade sculpted by Agostino di Duccio (1457-61); the evocative early-Christian church of San Michele Arcangelo (5th or 6th century); the church of Sant'Agostino and the Baroque oratory of Sant'Agostino in the underground rooms of which was recently discovered an early work by Raphael, who received his early training in Perugino's workshop. In the immediate surroundings is the *Volumni hypogeum*, an Etruscan underground tomb where the arrangement of rooms reproduces the layout of an ancient house.

Though it is a provincial town, Perugia has an active international cultural life and a pronounced international calling. Thousands of young people from around the world attend the Università per Stranieri, housed since 1926 in the rooms of Palazzo Gallenga Stuart. No less important is the Italian university which has been in existence since 1307. It is for young people that the important Umbria Jazz Festival which takes place in the second week of July, and the Sagra Musicale Umbra, in the first fortnight of September, are held.

61. The facade of the Oratory of San Bernardino in Perugia.

62. Agostino di Duccio: detail from the lunette of the main door with St Bernardine ascending to Heaven.

63. *Benedetto Bonfigli: standard of San Bernardino, detail showing the Oratory in the background. Perugia, Galleria Nazionale dell'Umbria.*

64. *Umbria Jazz concert.*

63

64

65

THE VALLE UMBRA

Its favourable geographical position and the importance of its towns have always made the Valle Umbra the heart of the region. On 16th-century maps, for example, the term Umbria was used to describe the duchy of Spoleto. In ancient times the Clitunno, Topino and Chiascio rivers formed one huge lake, the *Lacus Umber*, which occupied the whole of the valley floor. Large-scale reclamation projects were undertaken under the Romans in order to provide new farmland to allocate to war veterans as a reward for their services. The fields below Spello are still regularly arranged, divided by rows of poplars and 15th-century drainage ditches, in a repetition of the 1st century B.C. rural land division which followed the foundation of a colony of legionaries. The valley's strategic importance was increased by the Via Flaminia, along which the towns of Bevagna, Trevi and Foligno were founded. The consular road was linked to Etruscan Perugia by a road running along the side of Mount Subasio in the territory of Assisi and fording the Chiascio river near Bastia, the ancient *Insula Romana*, so

called because of the marshy state of the land. The agricultural crisis of the 1950's, the exodus from the countryside and the desertion of the mountains, combined with recent industrialization along the Via Flaminia and the ss. 75, have brought about a great change in the original landscape. A large part of the working population has been concentrated on the south side of the valley in an anonymous agglomeration of dwellings which runs without a break between Ponte San Giovanni and Trevi. The landscape at the foot of the Martani Hills, where the original agricultural calling of the Umbrians has survived, is still rural.

Among the new towns an increasingly important role has been played by *Bastia Umbra*, which preserves very little of its Roman foundation or medieval history. This heavily populated town is the home of important food and animal feed producers. The suburbs of Bastia which have grown a lot in

65. View of Foligno from Montefalco.

66

66. *View of Campello Alto with the Valle Umbra in the background.*

recent decades are now indistinguishable from those of the modern *Santa Maria degli Angeli*. The latter town grew up around the monumental basilica of Santa Maria degli Angeli, the large church commissioned by Pius V in 1569 as a copy of the Santa Casa in Loreto, to promote the indulgence of the Pardon which is received every year at the beginning of August. Beneath the fine dome designed by Galeazzo Alessi is the chapel of the Porziuncola, a small church restored by St Francis in 1206 where the saint founded the Order of Minor Friars and where he returned to die on 3 October 1226. In addition to the relics of the early Franciscan sites, the chapels of the Renaissance church are worth a visit. They house the richest collection of Umbrian painting from the period of the Counter-Reformation.

Once past the low hills separating the valleys of the Tiber and the Chiascio, the southern slope of the valley is dominated by the isolated massif of Mount Subasio with its unmistakable rounded form. The slope descends towards *Assisi*, built entirely of pink and white stone quarried from the hill. The ancient Umbrian settlement was situated on the level saddle between Mount Asio, where the citadel stood, and Mount San Rufino. Having become a Roman municipium, it flourished after the foundation of a shrine dedicated to the cult of the Dioscuri. The shrine was built on a series of terraces according to a design inspired by Greek models and adopted in numerous towns in Latium, for example, in Palestrina. At that time the town took on its characteristic stepped appearance, referred to by the ancient Roman poet Propertius, a native of Assisi. He writes that he was born "there where Bevagna, in the low plain, is enveloped in misty vapours, / while the Umbran lake is warmed beneath the summer sun, / and the walls of the great Assisi rise towards the summit, / walls rendered more famous by your genius". The ancient layout can still be seen in the medieval urban fabric which retained the original reinforcing embankments.

After the fall of the Roman Empire Assisi played a marginal role among the territories under the control of the Longobard duchy of Spoleto, but achieved universal prominence with the advent of Francis (1182-1226).

His decision to live in strict accordance with the message of the Bible won him a growing number of followers prepared to abandon their earthly possessions and embrace a poor, humble and chaste life. The construction of a sanctuary in honour of St

67. *Maestro di San Francesco: St. Francis. Museum of the Basilica of Santa Maria degli Angeli.*

68. *Niccolò di Liberatore, known as Alunno: predella with the Transfer of the Body of San Rufino, detail of Assisi. Assisi, Museo Capitolare.*

Francis and a church above the tomb of St Clair, the founder of the order of the Clarisse nuns, brought about a radical change in the town's compact layout, giving it its characteristic elongated form. The erection of new town walls in the early years of the 14th century determined its final shape. From 1319 on, violent struggles between opposing political factions brought about the rapid decline of Assisi and helped cause the extensive poverty from which

68

the town only recovered this century when modern means of transport encouraged mass tourism.

Nevertheless, despite the unseemly invasion by souvenir outlets which have chased away the old crafts shops, Assisi is more than a city of art. Its name evokes the messages of peace and love of nature which were proclaimed to the whole world by St Francis and which make it the heart of Christendom, second only to Rome. The Monastery is increasingly a point of reference for pacifist and ecological groups, giving a prophetic power to Dante's words when he wrote, in the XI Canto of Paradise: "Therefore let him who speaks of this place, say not Ascesi, for he would say little, but Orient, if he properly would speak", in reference to the universal import of St Francis' message.

The centre of the town is Piazza del Comune, situated at the intersection of the main streets. It stands on the site of a pagan sanctuary of which the so-called Temple of Minerva remains, whose praises were sung by the German poet Goethe. Against the columns of the pronaos stands the Torre del Popolo, completed in 1305, and the 13th-century Palazzo del Capitano del Popolo. The Roman piazza can still be seen beneath the medieval paving. Assisi's most famous monument, however, is the Basilica of St Francis (1228-1253), built in the Gothic style over the saint's tomb, which is constantly visited by pilgrims and tourists alike. The

prodigious cycle of frescoes decorating the walls, exalting the figure of St Francis and the mission entrusted to the religious order founded by him, make it the principal monument of medieval painting to be found in Italy. The execution of the work, under the direct control of the Holy See, was entrusted to the most important artists of the time, including Cimabue and Giotto from Florence, Torriti and the anonymous 'Maestro di Isacco' from Rome, and Simone Martini and Pietro Lorenzetti from Siena. There is an exuberance of form and colour in these frescoes which heralds the birth of Gothic naturalism.

The town has a typically medieval appearance, though exaggerated by the heavy restoration carried out in 1926 on the occasion of the 700th anniversary of Francis' death. The artistic patrimony accumulated over centuries has now slightly faded, but it must have been striking at the end of the 19th century when the French historian Ernest Renan remarked to a friend: "Assisi, my friend, is an incomparable place, and I have been amply repaid for the effort I made to visit it. Just think, the great popular legend of the Middle Ages depicted in its entirety in the two churches one above the other, painted by Giotto and Cimabue. The town is even more ancient than its monuments. It is completely medieval, with entire abandoned streets which have remained stone for stone as they were in the 14th

69

century... the profusion of art surpasses all imagination. The exteriors, interiors, doors, windows, beams and chimney-pieces of the houses are all painted and sculpted".

Buildings worthy of an attentive visit include the church of Santa Chiara (1257-1265), decorated by Umbrian masters, with the Crucifix which spoke to St Francis; the Romanesque cathedral of San Rufino, with its fine sculpted facade and the adjoining Museo Capitolare; the austere abbey of San Pietro; the Albornozian fort in a panoramic position at the top of the Asio hill, and the Franciscan sanctuaries of San Damiano and Le Carceri on the thickly wooded slopes of Mount Subasio.

Life is slow and lazy in the sunlit lanes and the green of the vegetable gardens where the cloisters of the monasteries and convents are often concealed. It comes alive on feast days, which are particularly impressive in Assisi since large numbers of people always take part. The most important dates commemorate the death of St Francis (3-4 October) and the Indulgence of the Pardon in the

69. View of Assisi.

70. The mighty arches of the San Francesco complex at Assisi.

71. The facade of the Basilica of San Francesco.

Porziuncola chapel (31 July-2 August). The Easter celebrations are particularly evocative. During the whole of Lent, in the lower church of San Francesco, the 'Funzione della corda pia' (Ceremony of the sacred rope) takes place in memory of Christ's death. Each Friday at sunset the friars walk in procession behind a roughly hewn cross, holding a rope around their necks; when they reach the chapel of the Crucifixion they kneel down and invoke the name of Christ, accompanied by plainsong.

The ceremony is repeated every Saturday in St

70

71

The Basilica of San Francesco

One can visit Assisi for religious reasons, to pray on the tomb of the best loved saint of western Christendom, or for love of art, to admire the extraordinary building erected as a crown over his tomb. Whether for reasons of Faith or of Art, Assisi is a fundamental halt on our spiritual path.

The idea of constructing the building, to be both the saint's tomb and the home of the Order of Minor Friars, came to Gregory IX against the conflicting views of the friars themselves. The pope himself laid the foundation stone on 11 July 1228, the day following the canonization of Francis, on a plot of steeply-sloping land at the lower edge of the Asio hill. For this reason the church is made up of two blocks, one above the other. The lower church, permanently immersed in half-light, appears as an enormous crypt, at the same time tomb-shrine and church of pilgrimage, and this is how it was used until the construction of a new crypt in 1822. The luminous upper church acts as a monastic choir, preaching hall and papal chapel.

On the vast walls of the upper church the life of the saint is illustrated for visiting pilgrims. Alongside are scenes from the life of Christ, on whose example Francis sought to model himself in all his acts. On either side of the nave are stories from the Old and New Testaments, symbolizing, in the exegesis of Gioacchino da Fiore, the first two ages of the world, that of the Father and that of the Son.

Below, the life of St Francis, divided into 28 episodes, is conceived as a gradual ascent to God, following the saint's renewal of the evangelical message. His figure appears in the stories from the Apocalypse in the north transept, where he is the embodiment of the angel of the sixth seal, the initiator of the age of the Spirit. In the stories from the life of Mary in the apse, Francis' devotion to the Virgin is exalted, while his obedience to the Church of Rome finds expression in the stories of the Apostles in the north transept. The fresco cycles covering the church's walls make it the most important monument in our understanding of Gothic painting in Italy. The immense task was carried out in the last quarter of the 13th century, and involved the greatest artists of the time, from Cimabue and Jacopo Torriti to the young Giotto, who took his first artistic steps in Assisi. In the presbytery of the lower church the theme of Francis' adherence to the word of the Bible appears again together with the role of the Order of Minor Friars who were charged with the task of completing the mission entrusted to Francis. Above the high altar are paintings of the *Glory of St Francis* and the three monastic vows, *Obedience, Poverty* and *Chastity,* placed in correlation with the stories of the *Childhood* and *Passion of Christ,* frescoed in the wings of the transept. The huge task was started by the workshop of Giotto, who made use of local collaborators, and was completed by the Sienese artist Pietro Lorenzetti in the second half of the 14th century. (See also the splendid frescoes by Simone Martini in the chapel of San Martino.)

I. *Interior of the Upper Church.*

II. *Maestro di San Francesco: St Francis Preaching to the Birds. Lower Church.*

III. *Jacopo Torriti: Separation of Light and Darkness. Upper Church.*

IV. *Cimabue: Fall of Simon Magus. Upper Church.*

V. *Giotto: The Simple Man's Homage to Assisi. Upper Church.*

VI. *Simone Martini: St Martin is Knighted, detail. Lower Church.*

VII. *Pietro Lorenzetti: Last Supper, detail. Lower Church.*

I

II

III

V

VII

72

74

Francis' tomb to commemorate the saint's death. On the evening of Easter Thursday the deposition of Christ is re-enacted in the cathedral: a 16th-century wooden Christ is removed from the cross and laid on a catafalque to be worshipped by the people. The next morning the catafalque is carried into San Francesco where it is joined in the evening by a statue of the Virgin Mary, carried in procession by priests and members of the confraternities dressed in sackcloth and bearing heavy wooden crosses on their shoulders. In complete silence the holy image is carried back to the cathedral through the torch-lit streets of the town. A totally pagan spirit is evoked by the 'Calendimaggio', a tournament in traditional costume saluting with songs and dances the return of spring.

At the other end of Mount Subasio stands *Spello*, a pretty town of Umbrian origin which became a Roman colony during the late Republican age. This period also saw the construction of the great civic monuments, the town walls and gates, the theatre and amphitheatre. A legend tells that the knight-errant Roland was held prisoner in the towers of the Porta di Venere; freed, as soon as his identity was revealed, he scornfully urinated against the town walls, opening up a large tunnel which is still marked today. Spello has many churches with a

72. Giotto: The Gift of the Cloak, detail of the town of Assisi. Upper Church of San Francesco.

73. A medieval lane in Assisi.

74. The 13th-century Convent of San Damiano on the slopes of Mount Subasio.

75. The Romanesque Cathedral of Assisi named after San Rufino.

76. The Church of Santa Chiara at Assisi.

77. Detail of the town of Spello in a painting by Marcantonio Grecchi, from the museum of Santa Maria Maggiore at Spello.

78. The Porta Venere at Spello.

76

wealth of works of art. A visit to the Cappella Bella (1501) by Pintoricchio, in the Romanesque church of Santa Maria Maggiore, should not be missed. This work is the masterpiece of this artist, who was the favourite painter of popes such as Alexander VI and Pius III. In Sant'Andrea there is also a Giottoesque *Crucifix*, painted by a bitter-sweet Umbrian follower of the Tuscan master. If we climb the steep steps to the Capuchin monastery dug out within the fort of cardinal Albornoz, we get (from beside a Roman arch reduced to no more than a thin bow across the sky) a delightful view of the Valle Umbra: the silver sheen of the olive groves on the Subasio, the small Romanesque church of San Claudio clinging to the ruins of the amphitheatre and the dark green of the cypresses in the park of Villa Fidelia. On the Sunday following Corpus Christi the town is decked out for the 'Infiorata': the streets are carpeted with floral compositions on religious themes, made during the night by all inhabitants of the town.

At the geometric centre of the Valle Umbra stands the town of *Foligno*, jokingly referred to in the colourful local dialect as 'lu centru de lu munnu', the centre of the world. The Roman *Fulgineum* was founded on the stretch of the Via Flaminia where the Valle Umbra and the valley of the Topino meet, near the present-day cemetery of Santa Maria in Campis. When the Roman Empire was in its death throes the inhabitants invoked the protection of the canonized Bishop Felicianus, and founded a new town next to his tomb along the Topino river. The young Frederick II of Swabia, who had been entrusted by Pope Innocent III to the care of Conrad of Urslingen, Duke of Spoleto, on the death of his parents Henry VI and Costance of Naples, stayed in the town. Loyalty to the imperial cause brought Foligno into disastrous conflict with the Guelf town of Perugia which twice, in 1253 and in 1282, laid siege to the town, diverting the course of the Topino and demolishing the walls. Under the rule of the Trinci family (1310-1439), the town was enriched with monumental churches and mansions. On its return to papal control, with the death of Corrado III Trinci by the hand of Cardinal Vitelleschi, Foligno became a thriving commercial centre thanks to its enviable position on the route between Rome and Ancona. The town was famous as the birthplace of Paoluccio Trinci, a hermit friar who reformed the Order of the Minor Friars and returned the members to a strict observance of the original Franciscan rules. It is also known for its 'fulignata', sweets made from sugar and almonds. The sweetmeat industry was well-known to travellers and "Foligno's sugar-paved streets" are recorded in a 16th-century sonnet describing the

77

most important towns in Italy. The liveliness of the local businessmen was responsible for the early introduction of the art of printing. Foligno was the third town in Italy, after Subiaco and Rome, to have a printing-press: the first edition of Dante's *Divine Comedy* was printed here in 1472. During the 17th century the austere facades of the patrician mansions on the most important streets were enriched as symbols of the wealth of a farming nobility which divided its time between trade and ceremony. The short-lived Baroque society founded the 'Giostra della Quintana' (Quintain Joust), a tournament in antique costume inspired by a riding competition of 1613 which sought to establish what was more important for an honourable knight, loyalty to his prince or to the lady of his heart. The competition is fought between ten riders representing the ten sections of the town, who test their skill in spearing with their lance a series of rings of ever smaller diameter from a galloping horse.

Foligno's historic appearance is unfortunately marred by the serious damage suffered during the last war and the rash rebuilding which followed. However, a walk through the maze of streets which have often been left abandoned and desolate can unearth pleasant surprises such as the beautiful 'Quartiere delle Conce', once inhabited by the

78

leather tanners (*concia*=tannery).

Noteworthy sights include Palazzo Trinci and the adjacent picture gallery in the central Piazza della Repubblica. The palazzo is one of the finest private mansions in central Italy, its large rooms decorated with profane scenes of the early 15th century. Also interesting are the Romanesque sculptures of the cathedral, the church of Santa Maria Infraportas with Romanesque and Renaissance frescoes, and the polyptychs by Niccolò di Liberatore in San Niccolò. On the slopes of Mount Serrone stands the abbey of *Sassovivo*, founded around 1000, with a cloister designed by the Roman architect Pietro di Maria (1229).

Once past Foligno the valley continues between the Supapennine peaks of Mount Brunetta and Mount Serrano to the east and the gentle slopes of the Martani Hills to the west. The modern ss. 3 grazes the southern side, while the Via Flaminia ran down the centre of the valley of the Clitunno river, where a continuous row of poplars can still be seen.

Only at the end of the 18th century did the medi-

79

80

79. The 16th-century tabernacle by Rocco da Vicenza from the altar of Santa Maria Maggiore.

80. Pintoricchio: Annunciation. Church of Santa Maria Maggiore, Baglioni Chapel.

81, 82. Pintoricchio: Adoration of the Shepherds, details. Church of Santa Maria Maggiore, Baglioni Chapel.

83. Villa Fidelia near Spello.

81

83

eval road take over from the ancient consular route; one of the first to comment on this was Johann Wolfgang Goethe as he journeyed towards Spoleto. Near Santa Maria di Pietrarossa, a country church entirely covered with 15th-century votive images, stood the staging post of *Trevi*, the Roman *Trebiae* which was moved to the summit of a low hill during the Longobard period. "This is a place with an unrivalled beautiful view, since it stands atop a hill and commands over that magnificent plain lying between Perugia and Spoleto..." (Cipriano Piccolpasso, *Le piante e i ritratti delle città e terre dell'Umbria sottoposte al governo di Perugia*, 1565). The Longobard court grew up following the contours of the hill. The town preserves an archaic feudal atmosphere, with the streets paved in a herring-bone brick pattern and lined with the 16th-century mansions of the Valenti noble family. In the Gothic church of San Francesco is a noteworthy 14th-century *Crucifix*. Also interesting are the frescoes by Perugino and Spagna in Santa Maria delle Lacrime, a Renaissance church founded by members of the Valenti family in honour of a miraculous holy image.

Access to the opposite side of the valley is overlooked by the small town of *Montefalco*, known as the 'Balcony of Umbria' for its panoramic position.

First a Roman villa and then a Longobard court, a history shared by many of the villages in the surrounding countryside, it preserves the memory of its former calling in the round piazza at the top of the hill, around which the medieval buildings stand. The castle got its present name only in 1250, perhaps for an imperial falcon kept by the commune, one of the birds so appreciated by the emperor Frederick II of Swabia, a skilled huntsman and author of a treatise on falconery. Montefalco was the birthplace of St Clair of the Cross, the most exalted of Umbria's mystics, who lived from her very earliest childhood in the convent which bears her name (Santa Clara della Croce). Visitors may admire the chapel of Santa Croce, adorned with lively 14th-century decorations depicting scenes from the saint's life. In the church of San Francesco, the home of the local picture-gallery, can be seen frescoes painted with zealous devotion by Benozzo Gozzoli, depicting the life of St. Francis (1452). They are perhaps the greatest works of this modest pupil of Fra Angelico, with the disarming simplicity of their airy landscapes populated with penitent friars who seem to come from the pages of a fairy-tale, unmindful of the solemn oratory of the Florentine humanists.

The art historian Bernard Berenson underlined

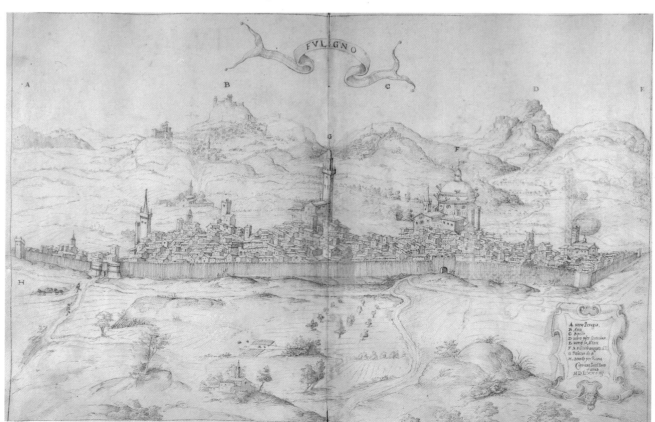

84. *Cipriano Piccolpasso, Le piante e i ritratti..., view of the town of Foligno. Perugia, Biblioteca Augusta, ms. 3064.*

85. *The Palazzo Comunale of Foligno with its 19th-century facade.*

86, 88. *The lateral facade of Foligno Cathedral with a detail of the Romanesque door.*

87. *A scene from the 'Giostra della Quintana' of Foligno.*

86

88

89

89. The "Portico delle Conce" at Foligno.

90. The Church of Santa Maria Infraportas at Foligno.

91. The 13th-century cloister of the Abbey of Sassovivo on the slopes of Mount Serrone.

92. Panoramic view of Trevi.

90

the importance of these frescoes to local painting, which was freed from a persistent medieval vision thanks to the help of Florence, with these rather harsh but accurate words: "Florence did not send to Umbria its greatest representative, nor even one of its greatest. Benozzo Gozzoli arrived here like a Roman proconsul who in his own country would have to have contented himself with a third or fourth grade post, but became a dazzling source of light in some distant Dacian or Briton province. And not only did Benozzo set in motion what little genius did exist in Umbria and provide models by which they could learn, he also taught the Umbrians to look to Florence for light and guidance".

91

92

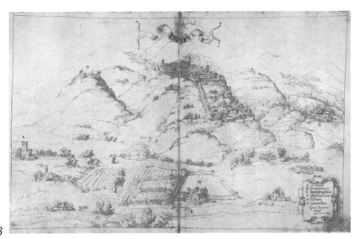

93

93. *Cipriano Piccolpasso, Le piante e i ritratti..., view of Trevi. Perugia, Biblioteca Augusta ms. 3064.*

94. *A lane in the medieval town of Trevi.*

95. *Perugino: Epiphany. Trevi, Church of the Madonna delle Lacrime.*

PETRVS·DE·CASTROPLEBIS·PINXIT·

TV·SOLA·IN·TERRIS·GENITRIX·ET·VIRGO·FVISTI·
REGINA·INCELIS·TV·QVOQVE·SOLA·MANES·

95

96. *The town of Monte-falco.*

97. *Benozzo Gozzoli: Birth of St Francis. Montefalco, Church of San Francesco.*

96

QVALITERB.F.FVITDENV̄TIATVS.A.ƆCP̄OIFŌMA.PEREGRINI.QVOD.DEBEBAT.NASCI.SICVT IPS.ISTABLO.QVALT.OVIDA.FATVV.P̄STĒNBA.BEVESIIIEÑ·IÑVA

97

98

98. Benozzo Gozzoli: Meeting of Francis with St Dominic; in the background a view of the Valle Umbra. Montefalco, Church of San Francesco.

99. The Tempietto del Clitunno.

From the top of its hill, however, Montefalco offers not only saints and painters (the secular poet Giosuè Carducci also sought inspiration in the pale visage of a Madonna by Francesco Melanzio). The vines besieging the houses yield a vigorous red wine called 'Sagrantino'. In winter the farmers hang the best bunches of grapes from the ceiling beams and draw from them an appetizing 'passito' (raisin wine), to be drunk with musk-fruits and 'pan nociato' biscuits, as bitter-sweet as the stories of St Francis frescoed by Benozzo. A Wine Week takes place in April, with the exhibition of typical local products.

On the sunny slopes of the hills olive trees have taken the place of the woods and vines have replaced wheat. From Trevi to Campello an ocean of olive-groves produces an excellently light and fragrant oil. In the countryside the days pass slowly, the rhythm of life marked by work in the fields. The landscape too seems immutable, and perhaps it is still the same as it was in ancient times. In the plain below Pissignano an early-Christian building stands beside the river: the celebrated *Tempietto del Clitunno*, where the laborious transition from the pagan temples to the basilicas of the new religion is revealed. The style of the portico imitates the structure in front of the pagan temples, which were reflected in the shallows of the famous Clitunno springs. Beneath the base a spring still gushes today whose name recalls the nymphs who lived in its

waters. In the hollow of the tympanum, however, among the vine-leaves and grapes, stands a cross, and on the architrave is carved an inscription dedicated to the "King of Angels". A few kilometres away, in the immediate environs of Spoleto, the church of San Salvatore shows itself even more faithful to the model of Roman civic basilicas. For this reason it was studied as an example of ancient architecture by the great master of the Renaissance, Francesco di Giorgio Martini. The *Clitunno Springs* have long since lost the Romantic charm which attracted travellers on their Grand Tour. No one looks here today for the pale oxen mentioned in the works of Roman poets. If anything, the springs offer weekend entertainment to those interested in the trout in the nearby lake.

"I ascended to Spoleto and went also to the aqueduct which at the same time is a bridge between one mountain and another. The ten arches built in brick spanning the whole valley stand firm against the passing of the centuries, while the water flows steadily throughout the year from one side of Spoleto to the other. This is the third construction of the ancients which I have before me and in which I can see the same majestic stamp. For the ancients the art of architecture was second nature, operating according to the usages and aims of the people. This is how the amphitheatre, the temple and the aqueduct appear. And it is only now that I feel with what justification I have always so de-

tested buildings constructed as if by caprice, such as the Winterkasten on the Weissenstein, for example: a nothing which serves no purpose, or at most an enormous chocolate-box. And the same can be said of a thousand other things: all still-born, since that which has within itself no real reason to exist has no life, cannot be great, and cannot become great". Goethe was moved to these thoughts by the sight of the arches towering over the sacred woods of Monteluco and the hill on which *Spoleto* stands. The German poet was unaware, however, of the bridge's medieval origins (it was built in 1282 to carry the water from the mountain into the town) perhaps because he was taken in by the inseparable blend of ancient and medieval in the layout of the town.

The town stands on the south-facing slope of the Sant'Elia hill, on the western extension of the Apennine range from which it is separated by the course of the Tessino torrent. Spoleto's history is closely linked to that of the mountain. The Flaminian consular road opened a path through the steep gorges carved out by the water and entered the town through the Porta Romana; it crossed the forum, the present-day Piazza del Mercato, and left the town through the Porta Fuga, continuing towards the valley of the Clitunno. The mountain above was traversed by numerous paths leading towards the Norcia and the Sabine territories. The site's strategic importance had already been noted by the ancient Umbrians who tried to protect the top of the hill, where the Gattapone fort now stands, with a wall built of large irregular blocks of stone (6th century B.C.). They were unable to defend themselves, however, from attack by the Romans and in 241 B.C. a colony of veterans was founded here; this colony displayed its loyalty to Rome by resisting Hannibal's assault after the Battle of Trasimene. The ancient layout can be easily identified by examining the medieval constructions which respected the regular arrangement of the *insulae*. These buildings sometimes included or took over the Roman buildings. See for instance, the temple beneath the church of Sant'Isacco or the house of Vespasia Polla beneath the Palazzo Comunale. After the fall of the Roman Empire the barbarian king Theodoric had the ancient buildings restored. The town's history continued under the Longobards who in 576 made it the head of a large duchy. When the sun set on the Longobard reign

100

Charlemagne turned it into a feudal possession and it remained under imperial control until the 12th century, when Innocent III claimed it as a possession of the Church. Spoleto's attachment to Rome caused Perugia to be preferred as the provincial capital after the unification of Italy. Spoleto's charm lies in its well-preserved urban layout and in the respect for historical forms and materials which make it a standard-bearer among Umbrian towns. The many noteworthy buildings in the old town centre include the Romanesque cathedral on the spectacular Piazza dell'Arengo, enriched with magnificent frescoes by Filippo Lippi, which have been excellently restored; the Rocca dell'Albornoz and

100. Spoleto dominated by the Rocca del Gattapone.

101, 102. Spoleto's two most famous monuments: the Ponte delle Torri and the Cathedral.

101

the 13th-century Ponte delle Torri; the church of San Pietro, with the Romanesque sculptures on its facade; the lively Piazza del Mercato above the Roman forum, with the Drusus Arch and the paintings in the crypt of Sant'Isacco (12th century); Sant'Eufemia and the adjacent Museo Diocesano, containing a wealth of paintings from the diocese, and the early-Christian church of San Salvatore.

Spoleto's fame is linked above all to the 'Festival dei due Mondi' (last week in June - second week in July), one of the few Italian cultural events enjoying international prestige, with plays, ballet, concerts and exhibitions. More refined palates will enjoy the 'Teatro Lirico Sperimentale' (late September) which is to be thanked for the discovery of many young opera singers.

Spoleto's cuisine is simple but full-flavoured; it is based on local ingredients such as olive oil and pecorino (ewe's milk cheese) or woodland products like black truffles, mushrooms and asparagus. Specialities include 'stringozzi', pasta served with black truffles, polenta with a sauce of sausages and pork rind, ragout of wood-pigeon, mutton chops, and truffle or herb omelettes. Puddings include Easter cakes, 'attorta' and 'crescionda'.

We return to Perugia by the east side of the valley, along a less busy but no less interesting road winding slowly between fields. The road passes the Ro-

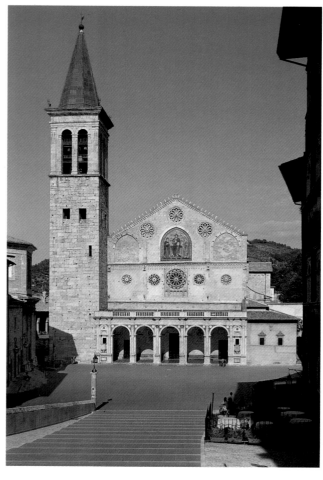

102

103, 104. *Filippo Lippi: Coronation and Death of the Virgin, frescoes in the apse of Spoleto Cathedral.*

103

104

106

105, 106. *The Fonte di Piazza at Spoleto, with a detail of one of the masks.*

107. *Detail of the splendid Romanesque reliefs decorating the facade of the Church of San Pietro at Spoleto.*

107

The Town of the Festival

In August 1956 the Veronese newspaper "L'Arena" published a long interview with Gian Carlo Menotti. The composer spoke of his "very interesting journey through most of Italy in search of the realization of a dream: to find a town, a small town, if possible free of cars and scooters, where he could establish an annual festival of chamber music, opera, chamber opera, drama, ballet etc. He visited dozens of towns, both small and medium-sized, avoiding the large towns, and became aware of the decline of Italian provincial theatre. He talked sadly of the jewels of theatre architecture falling into ruin, of disused theatres, of walls crumbling with the effects of time and negligence.

Menotti eventually found Spoleto, a quiet town with a theatrical tradition. It had initiated an Experimental Opera House and had already given Italy some excellent performers and launched several young people on the difficult musical path. 'In Spoleto', said Menotti, 'the mayor told me that if we hold a festival there, as I hope we will, not a single scooter will roar or buzz around or near the theatre: there will be total silence, peace!'»

The festival took place. After a year of preparation the curtain went up on 5 June 1958, with *Macbeth* by Giuseppe Verdi, produced by Luchino Visconti and under the musical direction of Thomas Schippers. There followed a full programme of ballet, concerts, drama and art exhibitions of the highest standard. It was further enlivened by social functions in the austere mansions of the quiet Umbrian town where high society from around the world had gathered. Menotti, born in Lombardy but a naturalized American, was then 45 years old and had considerable success on Broadway behind him as a composer of operas based on contemporary themes, for which he also wrote the librettos. From its first edition the Spoleto festival took on a sharp high-society tone and in a short time became an exclusive meeting place of society life, for those who loved to watch and to take part in the great theatre of the world.

For over thirty years the cobblestones of the medieval lanes, the melancholy piazzas and the crumbling plaster of the mansions and deconsecrated churches – picturesque feature and not sad abandon, since Spoleto was and is the worthy home of a restoration school – have been transformed into a shining international window, playing host on the venerable stage of the capital of the Longobard duchy to the most elegant avantgarde.

I. Concert during the 'Festival dei Due Mondi'.

manesque parish churches of San Brizio and Castelritaldi as it continues towards Montefalco, amidst olive-groves and the vineyards where Sagrantino is made. Entering the smaller valleys of the Martani Hills, which are crossed by the original Via Flaminia, the road passes through an enchanting rural landscape dotted with austere Romanesque abbeys built on the sites of the old staging-posts: San Felice di Giano, San Terenziano, Santa Maria di Viepri, Santi Fidenzio e Terenzio, Santa Illuminata and Santa Maria in Pantano.

In the plain below Montefalco stands the charming small town of *Bevagna*. Of Roman origin, it flourished until the 1st century A.D. when the increased importance of *Spoletium* and *Fulgineum* attracted trade elsewhere, diverting the route of the Via Flaminia and bringing about its rapid decline. The quiet enchantment of Piazza Silvestri, crowned with the severe facades of the Romanesque

108. View of Bevagna from Montefalco.

109. The fine Piazza Silvestri at Bevagna.

108

109

110. The door of the Church of San Michele at Bevagna.

111. The Etruscan tomb of Bettona.

110

churches of San Michele and San Silvestro, and by the shady arcade of the Palazzo Comunale, is enlivened on Sunday afternoon by the subdued bustle of old farmers, who hang around in the square with their crumpled felt hats in their hands talking about the price of wheat and the quality of grapes. They seem to have walked out of a photograph from the 1920's, so unlike scenes in the better-known towns of Italy. And from the outline of the houses the long curve of an amphitheatre comes into view, in the darkness of a cellar, the marble squares of a mosaic from a Roman bath shine out, and from the plaster walls of Sant'Agostino, the popular paintings of the Middle Ages emerge. This is the truer side of Umbria, the Umbria beloved of St Francis, who came to preach to the birds at nearby *Pian d'Arca*.

In the countryside around Bevagna all the rivers of the Valle Spoletana are gathered, the Topino, Clitunno, Teverone and Attone which, together with the canals dug in the 15th century to drain the marshes, make the land fertile. The fields are intensively cultivated and there are numerous pig-farms, although it is common to come across the ruins of farm-houses abandoned during the exodus from the land in the 1950's. The nearby town of *Cannara* is famous for its onions, and in September there is a gastronomic festival, the best of the thousands which take place throughout the countryside during the summer months. Far away against the backdrop of Mount Subasio stands Assisi. On the opposite hills is *Bettona*, overlooking the valleys of the Topino and the Tiber. The Umbrian town, anciently named *Vettona*, is still surrounded by its thick walls. Two paintings by Perugino can be seen in the local picture gallery.

THE VALLEY OF THE TIBER

A major feature of the Umbrian landscape is the flood plain of the Tiber, the longest river in central and southern Italy, which runs the region's entire length, from the Apennines above Sansepolcro to the border with Latium below Otricoli. For centuries the river was a vehicle of contact and trade – Pliny the Younger, who had a villa at San Giustino, tells that the river was navigable during the winter as far as Città di Castello – but was also an insuperable barrier between the Umbrians and the Etruscans, between the Longobard duchy and Perugia's territory. Today as in the past the river runs through not very extensive farmland which is, however, intensively cultivated with valuable crops favoured by the abundant supply of water for irrigation. Access to Umbria from the Po valley is via the valley of the Savio river, entered at Cesena. The old Tiberina trunk road winding along the hill-side repayed its inconvenience to travellers with the beauty of the views it afforded. It has now been replaced, without very much respect for the natural environment, by a fast two-way highway, the soon-to-be-completed ss. 3 bis, which crosses the whole region and joins the motorway at Orte. On this road we find *Sarsina*, founded by the ancient Umbrians, which was the birthplace of the comic poet Plautus. The Apennine watershed is crossed at Verghereto, in a harsh and majestic landscape dominated by the massif of Mount Fumaiolo on which is the catchment area of the Tiber.

This river, starting out as a mountain torrent, full and fast-flowing in winter and dry during the summer, suddenly opens out into a wide valley as far as Città di Castello, where the valley narrows into a gateway before widening again. The main town in the Tuscan stretch of the valley of the Tiber is *Sansepolcro*, a lively industrial town with a great artistic tradition, the birthplace of Piero della Francesca, Matteo di Giovanni, Santi di Tito and the Alberti family. No town in provincial Tuscany can boast a similar company. It is almost as if the clear air of the Casentino valley, where Michelangelo was also born, sharpened invention and skill. The town boasts a wealth of churches and mansions. There is an important picture gallery preserving, amongst other works, two masterpieces by Piero della Francesca. At nearby *Monterchi*, in the midst of fields of sunflowers, is a small chapel with the *Madonna del Parto*, a fresco by Piero della Francesca painted in memory of his mother who was born here.

Umbria begins at *San Giustino*, an agricultural

112. The Castello Bufalini of San Giustino in Valtiberina.

113

town which once belonged to the Bufalini family whose magnificent patrician home with rooms frescoed by Cristoforo Gherardi was recently purchased by the 'Comune'. The land is intensively cultivated, thanks to the breadth of the valley floor, mainly with sunflowers and corn. The area is traditionally known for the growing of tobacco which was introduced in 1575 and developed particularly in the free zone of *Cospaia*, a tiny suburb of San Giustino, which was not sold with Sansepolcro and survived as an independent republic until 1826 due to tobacco smuggling. Alongside the farm-houses one can still see the tall towers with the chimneys of the drying chambers.

Città di Castello is a lively small commercial town, with some important mechanical industries and an established printing tradition. Founded by the ancient Umbrians, it grew in importance under Roman rule until it became a municipium (1st century B.C.). At that time the town was called *Tifernum Tiberinum*, since it stood on the banks of the Tiber. This name survives in the name of the inhabitants, who are known as 'tifernati'. The Roman town was rectangular in shape, stretching

113. View of Città di Castello.

out along the Via Tiberiana, and remained so despite medieval changes when Castello consolidated its strategic role on the Byzantine corridor linking Rome to Ravenna. Under the rule of the Vitelli family (15th and 16th century), Castello was the scene of a lively court life and embellished with magnificent patrician mansions in the four districts of the town and new town walls. The town suffered considerable damage during the last war.

Rather than Città di Castello, this town in the upper valley of the Tiber might have been called Città di Raffaello, if a series of unfortunate events had not deprived it of almost all the works of art left here by the great painter from Urbino. After leaving the workshop of Pietro Perugino, Raphael's early works here included the *Altar-piece of San Nicola da Tolentino* for the Augustinians, now reduced to fragments and preserved in the museums of Capodimonte, Naples, the Tosio-Martinengo col-

115

116

114. *The Baroque façade of the Cathedral of Città di Castello.*

115. *The Palazzo del Podestà at Città di Castello.*

116. *Vasari's graffiti decoration on Palazzo Vitelli alla Cannoniera, which houses the Pinacoteca Comunale of Città di Castello.*

lection in Brescia, and the Louvre; the *Crucifixion* for the Gavari chapel in San Domenico, now in the National Gallery in London, and the celebrated *Marriage of the Virgin*, now hanging in the Brera Gallery in Milan. The latter was originally painted for the church of San Francesco. The only survivor is the timid gonfalon representing the *Trinity* and the *Creation of Eve*, an early work displayed in the frescoed rooms of Palazzo Vitelli alla Cannoniera, the home of the town's picture gallery. The town's artistic associations continue to this day, since it was the birthplace of Alberto Burri, perhaps the greatest living Italian artist. He has donated such a rich collection of works to his native town that they have been used to create two museums, one in Palazzo Albizzini, inaugurated in 1981, and the other more recent museum housed in the large spaces of the former tobacco factory.

Many other places are worth a visit. The cathedral of San Florido preserves a dramatic *Transfiguration of Christ* by Rosso Fiorentino (1529), and in the adjoining Museo del Duomo is the Canoscio Treasure, a collection of early-Christian Eucharist vases. The Palazzo dei Priori and Palazzo del Podestà were designed by Angelo da Orvieto (1322-1338), the great architect from Orvieto who designed the striking Palazzo dei Consoli in Gubbio. Garavelle is home to the Centro delle Tradizioni Popolari, housing exhibits from the peasant and artisan world. Local cultural events include the Chamber Music 'Festival delle Nazioni', from the end of August to the beginning of September, and a white truffle and woodland products market and festival in November for gastronomic enthusiasts.

South of Città di Castello the course of the Tiber narrows between two parallel ridges of hills. To the east we catch a glimpse of the medieval town of

117

120

117. Raphael: standard of the Trinity, detail with the Creation of Eve. Città di Castello, Pinacoteca Comunale.

118. One of the rooms of the Garavelle Agricultural Museum near Città di Castello.

119, 120. A room of Palazzo Albizzini, and the vast hall of the former Tobacco Manufacture showing the collection which Alberto Burri donated to Città di Castello.

121. The castle of Civitella Ranieri near Umbertide.

122. The tower of the 14th-century fort of Umbertide.

121

Montone, the birthplace of Braccio Fortebraccio da Montone, the great mercenary condottiere, who after taking control of Perugia failed in his attempt to conquer the Kingdom of Italy at the Battle of L'Aquila (1424). Towers and castles dot the surrounding hills. The most beautiful is the castle of *Civitella Ranieri*, whose proud appearance is the result of 16th-century alterations. In the valley lie the modern districts of Umbertide, the ancient town of Fratta, at one time on the border of Perugia's territory and now a small town devoted to various industrial activities, the most important of which is traditional high-quality ceramic production. Of the old town, badly damaged during the Second World War, there survive the 14th-century fort (1385) and the pretty San Francesco district, separated from the rest of the town by the Centrale Umbra railway line.

Once past Umbertide the valley widens and after

122

123

its confluence with the Assino torrent the meandering river slows its course. Over the last few decades the west bank has been gradually occupied by several populous towns (Ponte Pattoli, Ponte Felcino, Ponte Valleceppi and Ponte San Giovanni) running up towards the suburbs of Perugia. These towns grew up around the characteristic mill-towers and the ancient bridges linking them to the provincial capital which can be seen at the top of the hill. At Collestrada the Val Tiberina meets the Valle Umbra and the Chiascio river flows into the Tiber at Torgiano, below the sunny hills where 'Rubesco di Torgiano', one of the region's finest wines, is produced. *Torgiano* has a well-arranged wine museum in the cellars of the 17th-century Palazzo Graziani-Baglioni owned by the Lungarotti wine-makers. It contains objects connected with wine production and a collection of antique pottery, decorated with enological subjects.

Until 1860 much of the central Tiber valley belonged to the Perugian abbey of San Pietro and was subject to frequent floods due to the river's changeable course. To escape this problem the medieval towns grew on the tops of the hills. Perhaps the most suggestive is *Deruta*, famous for its traditional pottery decorated with grotesque motifs. In the town hall is an important collection of Renaissance ceramics, together with two paintings by Niccolò di Liberatore, and the 17th-century canvases of the Lione Pascoli collection. The church of San Francesco preserves an early fresco by Pietro Perugino who left his earliest work, dated 1478, in

nearby *Cerqueto*. Along the road in the valley there are a great number of craft workshops producing decorative majolica, an important source of income for the local economy. Outside the town is the church of the Madonna di Bagno whose walls are entirely faced with hundreds of votive majolicas from the 17th and 18th centuries.

The ss. 3 bis continues south towards Rome, running along the east bank of the Tiber and avoiding the towns. The lower end of the valley is marked by the Todi hill, around which the river makes a wide curve towards the west, flowing through the Forello gorges. Against the horizon the harsh outline of *Todi* stands out sharply, suspended between the land and the sky like those miniature cities held in the palms of patron saints in 15th-century polyptychs. Wherever one looks, Todi offers a different aspect, like the skin of an old man marked by time.

The three lines of walls encircling it, Umbrian, Roman and medieval, recall the site's strategic importance, situated between Etruria and the Umbrian pastures (the Umbrian name 'Tuder' means frontier land). The town's importance grew due to the increased role of the Via Amerinia after the decline of the Cassia and Flaminia following the Longobard conquest. The pointed spire of San Fortunato marks the town's veneration of its patron saint, to whom Todi was to dedicate a magnificent church built on the site of the ancient Umbrian capitol. The perfect semi-spherical dome of Santa Maria della Consolazione records the attempt by its

124, 125. Two examples of the ceramic art of Deruta: ex-voto with a man struck by a thunderbolt and a dish with the profile of Caesar.

124

125

humanist architect to recreate on earth the heavenly vault: it rises gloriously against the azure sky with the same grace as the hills surrounding the rock. The design has been attributed to Donato Bramante, in the same years in which he was completing the design of the new St Peter's in Rome for Pope Julius II. Todi's history returns insistently to the Middle Ages when as the head of Umbria's Ghibelline towns its greatest buildings were erected: the beautiful main square with the Palazzo Comunale and the cathedral, the lower-class districts, the churches and the convents. At this time Todi was also home to the rough genius of Jacopone, the most intense 14th-century religious poet in Italy.

According to the legend of his conversion, Jacopone was a rakish lawyer who changed his life when he discovered that his wife, who died when the floor collapsed during a party, was wearing a hairshirt against her naked skin. His passionate verses display the scorn for worldly things expressed by the Umbrian Flagellants, who had taken to the streets after the example of Ranier Fasani of Perugia, combined with St Francis' unbounded love of creation: "Oh joy of the heart, which makes us sing of love! When joy bursts forth, it makes men sing, and their tongue stutters and knows not what it says; It cannot hide this sweetness inside!"

The historic town centre has a slightly decaying appearance, but it is entirely free of the horrors of modern buildings, perhaps because the exodus of inhabitants to the small outlying towns redirected the available money away from the centre. It is in the towns in the valley that the few factories in this mainly agricultural area have appeared. The hub of life in the town is Piazza Vittorio Emanuele, one of the most harmonious squares in Italy, built on the site of the ancient forum and surrounded by the spectacular backdrop of the cathedral (mid-13th century), the Romanesque Palazzo del Popolo (1214-1267), the Gothic Palazzo del Capitano del Popolo (1293-1297) and the Palazzo dei Priori (1337-1347), which has on its facade the heraldic emblem of Todi, an eagle, cast in bronze by Giovanni Giliacchi (1339).

Another important monument in the town is the Franciscan church of San Fortunato, begun in 1292.

126, 127. *Two views of Todi: perched on its hill and seen from above.*

128. *The elegant proportions of Santa Maria della Consolazione, just outside the inhabited area of Todi.*

126

127

129

130

129. Detail of one of the capitals of Todi Cathedral.

130. The artificial lake of Corbara.

131. Gubbio, with the unmistakable outline of Palazzo dei Consoli.

The interior is an aisleless nave and in one corner is a radiant Madonna by Masolino da Panicale. Walking along the steep lanes between the concentric circles of the walls one can see the Roman travertine blocks amongst the stones of the medieval houses in Piazza del Mercato, or the cavea of a theatre; descending into the Romanesque crypt of Santa Maria in Camuccia one is confronted by the remains of Roman mosaics and houses.

Having circled the hill, the Tiber continues its lazy course between the steep walls clad with holm-oak of the Forello gorge, carved out of the limestone rock of the Mount Peglia-Mount Croce ridge. It then flows into the artificial lake of Corbara, a popular site for anglers attracted by the good supply of carp and pike. West of the dam, the road passes the Franciscan convent of Pantanelli founded by St Francis in 1216. After its confluence with the Chiani river, the Tiber turns south-west and enters a Latian landscape at the border between the two regions.

THE AREA OF GUBBIO AND GUALDO TADINO

An age-old historical tradition links the Umbrian towns on the Apennines with the bordering region of the Marches. For centuries the mountain range was more an element of union than one of division, when mountains played an important economic role with stock-raising and cultivation of the woods. The numerous passes across the Apennines – Bocca Trabaria, Bocca Serriola, the Scheggia pass, Fossato di Vico, the Cornello pass, the Colfiorito plain – allowed trade to flourish between the river valleys of the inland Marches and papal Rome. The absence today of an efficient link between the two regions, except for the Rome-Ancona railway line, does not afford the same ease of communication. Before submitting to Antonio da Montefeltro in 1394, the town of Gubbio, checked to the west by the power of Perugia, had ventured into the Marches, conquering Cantiano and founding Pergola.

The most popular itinerary follows the old route of the Via Flaminia which leaves the Adriatic coast at Fano and crosses the Apennines at *Scheggia*, a Roman town on the Flaminia destroyed by the Hungarians in 927. The town stands at the base of the Catria massif, the sacred mountain of the ancient Umbrian people who had erected there a shrine dedicated to Jove. With the spread of Christianity, the mountain became home to a community of hermits. In 979 the nobleman Lodolfo Pamphily of Gubbio founded the monastery of *Fonte Avellana* amidst the green woods. This monastery became famous under the abbot Pier Damiani, a respected adviser to popes who was immortalized by Dante in Canto XXI of Paradise. The hilly slopes shelter the abbeys of Santa Maria di Sitria, founded by St Romuald in the early 11th century, and Sant'Emiliano in Congiuntoli (13th

132

132. *View of Gubbio from above.*

133. *A lane in the medieval town of Gubbio.*

134, 135. *The courtyard of the Palazzo Ducale in Gubbio, and the Largo del Bargello with the "Fonte dei Matti".*

133

135

century), and the hermitage of Monte Cucco (12th century).

From Scheggia we leave the Via Flaminia and take the panoramic s. 298 to *Gubbio*. Once over the Madonna della Cima pass, the road descends through thick pine-woods along the course of the Camignano torrent, which in its last stretch carves a route between two sheer cliffs. Large amounts of iridium, a rare mineral found particularly in meteorites, have been found in the rocks of the gorge. The presence of this iridium has been explained by American scientists as the result of the impact of an enormous meteorite. This would have raised a huge cloud of dust, obscuring the sun for some time; its impact would have had a destructive force equal to that which caused the dinosaurs to disappear from the face of the earth. Gubbio stands at the mouth of the gorge, on the sunny slopes of Mount Ingino at the edge of the flood plain of the Assino torrent.

If this was the route followed by the dukes of Urbino on their move to their summer residence, Gubbio must have been designed to be enjoyed in a bird's eye view from the Piccione Hills towards Perugia. From this angle the elongated outline of the lines of stone houses appears to be dominated by the imposing bulk of the Palazzo dei Consoli and Palazzo del Podestà, which act as the town's ideal centre of gravity. In the turbulent political climate of the early 14th century, with the attempt for control by the Gabrielli family and the final surrender to the Montefeltro, the seat of administrative and political power was built atop an artificial terrace in *locis que tangant omnia quarteria* (as written in the construction plans of the new public buildings – 14 December 1321), so as not to displease the opposing factions in the town. The

raised piazza which was created, enclosed between the harmonious facade of the Palazzo dei Consoli and the bright background of the countryside, inspired Federico da Montefeltro, a native of Gubbio, in his plan to create in Urbino "a town in the form of a palace" (Baldassar Castiglione, *The Courtier*), the prototype of all the ideal towns of the Renaissance. Gubbio is thoroughly medieval. The appearance of the primitive Umbrian town can be gleaned from an uncertain deciphering of the religious text engraved on the *Iguvine Tables*, seven bronze plates engraved in Umbrian and Latin describing the ritual processions at the three town-gates, the Veia, Trebulana and Tessenaca. Under Roman rule the town grew at the foot of Mount Ingino, with the foundation of a colony of veterans and the construction of important buildings such as the extant large theatre (1st century A.D.). After the fall of the Roman Empire, however, the absence of town walls led the remaining inhabitants to concentrate themselves around the early cathedral of San Mariano, along the course of the Cavarello torrent and in the noble quarter of San Martino. Destroyed by the Hungarians (917), the town rose again around the figure of the canonized Bishop

136

136. The Church of San Francesco at Gubbio.

by steep lanes. The historic centre is the majestic Piazza della Signoria, a man-made terrace at the edge of the four administrative districts into which the town is divided. On the square stand the Palazzo dei Consoli (1333-37), housing an archaeological museum and the picture gallery, and the unfinished Palazzo del Podestà, the seat of the council. On the side looking towards the hill, stands the neo-classical Palazzo Ranghiasci.

Further uphill is the Romanesque cathedral of San Mariano, with the fine Museo Capitolare next door. Directly opposite stands the Palazzo Ducale, adapted by Francesco di Giorgio Martini for Federico da Montefeltro (1476) on the site of the first town hall. The unusual asymmetrical courtyard and the ground floor rooms, unfortunately stripped of their Renaissance furnishings and the beautiful marquetry of the 'studiolo' (now in the Metropolitan Museum in New York), are open to the public. As we walk through the streets we can see other civic buildings. In the San Martino quarter is the Romanesque Palazzo del Capitano, opposite which a large stone embedded in the street marks the position of an Umbrian altar. In Via dei Consoli is the Gothic Palazzo del Bargello (1302), in front of which stands the 'Fonte dei Matti', a fountain so named because, according to tradition, whoever walked three times around the fountain has the right to the 'battesimo di matto', the 'baptism of the insane'. According to this late 19th-century custom, caps were distributed in the church of Sant'Ubaldo as cures for madness. The many churches in the town include the abbey of San Pietro, founded in the early Christian period but altered several times in the Middle Ages and during the Renaissance; the Gothic-style San Francesco (1259-92), preserving traces of 13th-century decoration, and the churches of Sant'Agostino and Santa Maria Nuova frescoed by Ottaviano Nelli.

Though it is situated far from the Via Flaminia, Gubbio controlled traffic along the road by means of a network of fortifications. *Costacciaro* is a medieval castle in a strategic position beside the Chiascio river. In 1477 the town was fortified by Francesco di Giorgio Martini for Federico da Montefeltro, since it was the first point of defence for the duchy of Urbino against those coming from Rome. Behind Costacciaro is Mount Cucco (1566 m), one of the most beautiful hills in the Umbrian Apennines and a favourite spot for hikers. The slopes and valleys are clothed in thick vegetation, with tall beech woods watered by numerous rivers and streams. The abundant water supply, exploited

Ubald who ordered the enlargement of the walls and the construction of a new cathedral near the top of the hill. The urban fabric is admirably well-preserved and so perfect that standing in the stone-paved streets the deep silence creates the impression that the town has been abandoned by its inhabitants. And yet the howling of the wolf tamed by St Francis still echoes through the streets on 15 May each year, when the silence is roughly broken by the Feast of St Ubald and the 'Corsa dei Ceri' (see also p. 97).

The remarkable level of preservation was caused not least by the poverty of the inhabitants under the rule of the Church, when the economy was based mainly on agriculture in an area where the land was poor and unprofitable, as well as by limited building. The crisis in the share-cropping system after the Second World War brought about the exodus of over 10,000 emigrants, and this loss was only righted in recent years by the opening of two cement factories exploiting a local source of klinker and by the increasing role of tourism.

Gubbio is based on a regular plan, with wide streets following the contours of the hill and linked

The 'Ceri' of the Patron Saint

If there is one festival where primitive pagan customs survive most strongly and the distinction between sacred and profane appears most ambiguous, it is during the 'Corsa dei Ceri' in Gubbio. The religious celebrations, originally to pay homage to the patron saint Ubaldo, with the usual offering of wax, are mixed with the complex ceremony of the «purification» of the town described in the Iguvine Tables, and folkloric tradition of the May-pole, symbolized by the shape of the 'Ceri'. The Ceri are three hollow wooden constructions about four metres tall and weighing over 400 kilogrammes, made up of two octagonal prisms linked by a long antenna. During the year the Ceri are kept hung up in the church of Sant'Ubaldo at the top of Mount Ingino, but during the race they are attached upright onto a litter supported by ten bearers known as 'ceraioli', led by a 'capodieci'. Originally the Ceri were carried by members of guilds of craftsmen, indicated by the statues crowning the spire: St Ubaldo for the Cero of the builders, St George for the artisans and traders, St Antony Abbot for the Cero of the peasants. The festival takes place on 15 May each year, the eve of St Ubaldo's day. At dawn the 'capitani' are awoken by drummers in period costume. All the Ceri-bearers gather in the church to take part in Mass and to choose the names of the 'capitani' who will assume their role two years later. There follows a short procession carrying the statues of the saints to the Palazzo dei Consoli, where the ceri have already been brought on the first Sunday in May. At midday the raising of the three ceri takes place outside the palazzo, preceded by the throwing of three amphoras into the jostling crowd of people who pick up the broken pieces as good luck charms. On a sign from the 'capitano' the bearers take hold of the long poles and run three laps around the square; they then divide into three processions to run through the streets, accompanied by singing and rowdy drinking. The climax of the festival takes place in the late afternoon. After a religious procession in which all the clergy and the bishop with a reliquary of St Ubaldo take part, the bishop blesses the Ceri and then a headlong race, often marked by dangerous falls, crosses the town and returns the Ceri to Piazza della Signoria before the final ascent of the steep slopes of Mount Ingino.

I, II. Gubbio's traditional 'Corsa dei Ceri'.

II

137. Nocera Umbra, an ancient town in its panoramic position.

138. Niccolò di Liberatore, known a. Alunno: polyptych, detail of the Nativity. Nocera Umbra, Pinacoteca Comunale.

139, 140. Examples of the great ceramic tradition of Gualdo Tadino.

by the Perugia aqueduct, has caused extensive karstenite formations within the mountain. Not far from the summit is the mouth of the Mount Cucco grotto, 922 m deep and more than 27 km long, one of the most important in Italy. The summit is popular among hang-gliding enthusiasts who make use of the strong rising air currents.

At *Fossato di Vico* the Flaminia meets the s. 76 from the valley of the Esino, a major road crossing the centre of the Marches and running towards Ancona, passing through Fabriano and Jesi. The town preserves an attractive medieval appearance and the chapel of the Piaggiola, entirely decorated with frescoes by Ottaviano Nelli (15th century).

Gualdo Tadino stands on a rise on the slopes of Mount Serra Santa at the edge of a wide valley irrigated by some tributaries of the Chiascio river. The ancient Tadinum was an important halt on the Flaminia, and for this reason was sacked several times around the time of the fall of the Roman Empire. In 552 it was the scene of the Battle of Tagina, when General Narses defeated the Goth army under Totila, opening the way for the Byzantine reconquest of Italy. The medieval town was rebuilt on Sant'Angelo hill (1237), taking the name Gualdo, the Longobard word for wood.

Gualdo Tadino is not a pretty town. The modern districts spreading out in the valley and the discredited new building developments in the old town centre have irremediably defaced its features. It is a great pity since Gualdo boasts a long and respected tradition in the production of decorative pottery (every summer an international ceramics competition is held here) and was the birthplace of an important painter from the early Renaissance in Umbria, Matteo da Gualdo. Interesting sights include the former cathedral of San Benedetto (1256), once a Benedictine monastery, and the Gothic church of San Francesco, decorated with frescoes by Matteo da Gualdo (15th century). At the top of the hill is the Flea fort, constructed by Frederick II of Swabia in 1242 and enlarged by Biordo Michelotti in 1394.

At *Nocera Umbra* the Via Flaminia met a consular

139

140

shortcut which crossed the Apennines at the Cornello pass and led to Loreto, a popular pilgrimage site in the 16th century for visitors to the Santa Casa shrine. The town follows the contours of a hill looking onto the valley of the Topino between the Pennino and Subasio hills. An Umbrian and then Roman town, it grew in importance under the Longobards, as testified by the rich collections of grave goods discovered in the necropolises and preserved in the Museo dell'Alto Medioevo in Rome. In 1248 the town was razed to the ground by the troops of Frederick II. It subsequently passed under the control of nearby Foligno.

The rule of the Trinci family was marked by an unhappy event which took place in the castle that stood beside the cathedral, of which there survives a tower. On the night of 10 January 1421 the lord of the castle, Pasquale di Vagnolo, caught Niccolò Trinci in bed with his wife; he hurled him from a window of the castle into the ravine below, and killed his brother Bartolomeo. Corrado Trinci escaped death and with the help of Braccio Fortebraccio reconquered the castle, throwing the unfortunate Pasquale di Vagnolo from the ramparts and killing over 150 of his servants.

THE AREA OF TERNI AND AMELIA

In modern, as in ancient times, a traveller arriving in Umbria on the Via Flaminia from Rome finds himself immediately in the district of Otricoli at the edge of the Sabina area. The opening of the 'Autostrada del Sole' in 1964 transferred the entrance to the region to the foot of the volcanic outcrop of Orte, where the swirling waters of the Nera slow down as they leave the gorges below Narni and flow into the Tiber. At the confluence of the two rivers the motorway meets the ss. 204 from Terni and heads towards Viterbo in Tuscia. The road and railway have riddled the valley with industrial factories and warehouses. This environmental defacement has spoiled even the magnificent appearance of Orte, which now overlooks a mass of anonymous blocks of flats from the top of its solitary hill. After entering Umbria the two-way highway runs alongside the Nera Montoro chemical works towards Narni, which is heralded by a large stone quarry. If there is time available, the disadvantages of the old Roman road are amply outweighed by the beauty of the rural landscape and the Romanesque churches perched above the Nera. A small gem is San Pudenziana at Visciano, built with blocks of travertine stripped from nearby Roman tombs.

Continuing as far as *Otricoli*, we visit the ruins of the riverside port populated by the Romans with the inhabitants of the nearby Umbrian castle who were deported at the time of the Social War (90 B.C.). The archaeological excavations were set under way in 1776 by Pope Pius VI and unearthed a wealth of material including a bust of Jove copied from a 4th-century B.C. Greek statue. In this abandoned and desolate scene, among the brambles and planted fields, one can make out the brick skeleton of a Roman bath, the basilica and the amphitheatre. Encircled by a wall at the top of the hill stands the restored early-Christian church of Santa Maria.

Overlooking a precipice is *Narni*, a knot of churches and ragged houses bunched closely together so as not to slip into the waters of the Nera below. The Umbrians founded a fortified enclosure here which the Romans destroyed (300 B.C.) and then rebuilt, before launching themselves into their conquest of the region. The Via Flaminia ran along the entire length of the rocky spur, before crossing the Nera river over a tall bridge (27 B.C.). Its strategic position at the entrance to the Terni basin made Narni a bulwark of defence for Rome and

141. The head of the Otricoli Jove, a copy of a Greek statue of the 4th century BC, today in the Vatican Museums.

thus saw itself involved in the Second Punic War and the barbarian invasions. The Romantic appeal of invincible nature and the majestic ruins of the bridge have attracted travellers and artists for centuries. Turner and Corot have painted splendid views of this place.

This warlike calling has impregnated the misty rows of houses; it has taken shape in the chivalric and courtly subjects of the reliefs on the facade of the Palazzetto Comunale; it has witnessed the birth of famous condottières such as Erasmo da Narni, known as Gattamelata (1370-1443), a captain of the Republic of Venice immortalized by Donatello in the celebrated equestrian monument in the Piazza del Santo in Padua; and it is renewed every year in the 'Corsa dell'Anello', a test of skill consisting in spearing with a lance a ring suspended on two strings between the houses at the beginning of Via Maggiore. The town is divided into three districts ('terzieri') which keenly compete for the prize.

The Roman and medieval town, crossed by the Via Flaminia, is centred around Piazza dei Priori, adorned with a polygonal fountain (1301) similar to the one in Perugia but without sculptural decoration, in which are reflected the Palazzo del Podestà (13th century), and the Loggia dei Priori (14th century) flanked by the Torre Civica. The Romanesque cathedral of San Giovenale (1145) was built against the first circle of walls, thereby enlarging the district of Mezule which occupies the side of the hill culminating in the Rocca Albornoziana. At the opposite end is the Santa Maria district, centred on the church of San Domenico, which houses the local picture gallery.

In the years after the First World War the beginnings of an industrial base at Narni Scalo for the production of electrodes and linoleum were followed by the gradual depopulation of the old town centre and the chaotic growth of workers' homes alongside the railway.

On top of a hill a short distance from Narni stands the ancient Umbrian town of *Amelia*. This elegant

142, 143. The Ponte di Augusto at Narni, in a contemporary photograph and in a painting by Corot at the Louvre.

142

143

144

145. Domenico Ghirlandaio: Coronation of the Virgin. Narni, Palazzo Comunale.

146. The Romanesque bell-tower of Amelia.

145

14

town suffers from an isolated position (though rumour has it that in the 19th century the inhabitants opposed the building of a railway line here so as not to disturb the passage of the doves, served in a delicious stew in the local trattorias), and yet a glance at the imposing walls of large blocks of stone encircling the whole hill is enough to make the visitor feel the weight of history. Amelia was an important halt on the Via Amerina, the military road linking Perugia to Rome via Vulci; after the Via Flaminia fell into disuse following the Longobard occupation of Spoleto, it became part of the Byzantine Corridor along which all trade between Rome and the Exarchate passed. It continued to expand until the loss of interest in the Via Amerina caused its present state of decay; with an economy anchored to agriculture alone this decline is still visible today.

The narrow lanes of the town follow the contours of the hill, passing beside architraves and other Roman fragments mixed with medieval towers and striking Renaissance mansions. These latter date from the time when the local prelates carried weight in the Holy See and could afford to commission sculptors such as Agostino di Duccio, the creator of the Geraldini chapel in San Francesco (1477), and when a local painter, Piermatteo d'Amelia, was appointed by Sixtus IV to decorate

148

149

the ceiling of the Sistine Chapel, before Michelangelo painted his Genesis. At the top of the hill stand the cathedral, with a neo-classical interior, and the tall polygonal bell-tower (1050). All around the deep green of the woods and the bubbling water of the torrents reign supreme.

After leaving Amelia, travellers can follow the ss. Amerina for a while, running along the eastern slope of the valley of the Tiber and passing through small towns submerged in an ocean of olive-groves and vineyards. The view stretches off into the distance to the wide horizon and on clear days reaches as far as the Cimino and Soratte hills beyond the border with Latium and Mount Amiata in Tuscany. *Lugnano in Teverina* boasts one of the finest Romanesque churches in Umbria (12th century), preceded by a porch with sculptural and mosaic decorations in the architrave which betray its debt to models from Latium. The town of *Alviano* is dominated by a large fort rebuilt in 1495 by Bartolomeo d'Alviano, a condottiere and humanist in the service of the Venetian republic; in the basement rooms is housed a museum on rural life and traditions. The parish church preserves an altar-piece by Niccolò di Liberatore (late 15th century) and an excellent fresco by the great painter Giovanni

150

Antonio de Sacchis, known as Pordenone after his native town. The fresco was executed around 1516 for Pentesilea Baglioni, the widow of Bartolomeo d'Alviano. In the valley the Tiber is blocked here by a dam producing hydroelectric power. The large lake has become the first wildlife reserve in Umbria, run by the WWF, and attracts numerous species of migrating birds.

After Narni the Roman Via Flaminia forked; the older route crossed the Nera over the Augustus Bridge, passed through *Carsulae*, the present-day San Gemini, and continued through the Martani Hills in the direction of Bevagna. The later route ran alongside the river as far as Terni and from there continued to Spoleto via the Somma pass. The Terni basin is a flood plain surrounded by mountains on all sides formed at the confluence of the Serra torrent and the Nera river. At the *Marmore waterfalls* the Velino flows into the Nera over a spectacular waterfall 165 m tall, created artificially by the consul Manlius Curius Dentatus (271 A.D.) to allow for the outflow of the still waters of the Rieti valley.

The abundant water supply – the Latin name *Interamna* means "town between the waters" – for the production of electrical energy at low cost led

151

152

the Ministry of War of the newly-founded Italian state to site a weapons factory here (1875), protected from possible enemy attack by its distance from the border and the sea. Immediately afterwards a steel-works and some factories producing carbide and ammonia were opened, making Terni the most important centre of the steel and chemical industries in pre-industrial Italy. Within only a few decades the new town had attracted a large part of the working population to the factories causing the depopulation of the mountain areas.

Its unattractive modern appearance, the result of the very serious damage suffered during the Second World War, means that *Terni* has no place on the

153

usual tourist routes in the region. Yet the town has an ancient history, documented by the prehistoric discoveries in the nearby necropolises. Founded by the Umbrians and then a thriving Roman municipium – the emperor M. Claudius Tacitus (275-276) was born here –, it preserves the foundations of the walls and the amphitheatre (32 A.D.). During the barbarian invasions it suffered devastating attacks and the population decreased so severely that it lost its bishop's see.

Destroyed several times in the Goth-Byzantine war (546, 554), razed to the ground by the Holy Roman Emperor Frederick I of Swabia (1174), it rose again as a free city. The town's most important historic buildings date from this period: the cathedral of Santa Maria Assunta with its Baroque interior (1653), the evocative church of San Salvatore (11th century) founded on the site of a pagan temple, the convent of Sant'Alm with 14th-century frescoes and the Paradisi chapel in the church of San Francesco, frescoed by Bartolomeo di Tommaso of Foligno (1449).

The great importance of mechanical industry in Terni's economy has not, however, suffocated the original peasant roots which reflower at the end of April with the 'Cantamaggio', a festival celebrating the return of spring with the singing of 'stornelli'.

Rustic tradition is the basis of local cooking too, with dishes such as 'ciriole', a flour and water pasta seasoned with oil, garlic and chilli peppers, and 'panpepato', which is eaten at Christmas time, a cake made of honey, almonds and chocolate, seasoned with spices and pepper.

In the verdant hills surrounding Terni are some attractive small towns with suggestive medieval appearances, in striking contrast with the chaotic industrial centre. The mountains around Terni are a paradise for hikers, offering the greatest concentration of signposted walking routes in the whole region and passing through spots of natural and artistic interest. If time is available, it is well worth going up to *Stroncone*, a short distance from the watershed with the Rieti basin, from where the Franciscan monastery of Greccio can be easily reached on foot. This monastery is closely linked to the memory of St Francis, who created the first nativity crib here. Another interesting spot is the surprising little village of *Miranda* situated on the top of a small hill overlooking the whole valley, where bread is still baked in raised wood-fired ovens. Another pleasant hike can be made to the lake at *Piediluco*, beyond the Marmore waterfalls, the largest lake in the Rieti plateau and the second largest in Umbria, after Lake Trasimene. Its waters

154

are cool, clear and calm, ideal for rowing competitions. The village is dominated by the ruins of the fort built by cardinal Albornoz in 1364.

From Terni one can follow for a stretch the early route of the Via Flaminia towards Todi. The modern ss. 3 bis crosses the 'Terre Arnolfe' area, named after the Germanic feudal lords who controlled it for a long time. The main town was *Cesi*, on the slope of Mount Torre Maggiore, where there is a precious altar-piece (1308) by an anonymous painter from Spoleto. At the top of the hill, near the Sant'Erasmo hermitage, are remains of imposing walls of large irregular blocks of stone dating from the 4th century B.C. which were part of a rural settlement identified as *Clusiolum*. This town was founded by Umbrians who had fled Narni after the Roman conquest.

In the fields on the valley is the archaeological site of *Carsulae*, whose history is closely tied to that of the Via Flaminia which crossed the town and of which a stretch has been unearthed. A prosperous Roman municipium, it drew its wealth from its vineyards and the nearby hot springs of San Gemini, celebrated since ancient times for their therapeutic properties. The absence of fortified walls made it easy prey during the first Goth invasions, but it was probably abandoned after a devastating earthquake and the diverting of traffic to the new stretch of the Via Flaminia to Spoleto. Buried for centuries beneath flood deposits and sacked for building materials, Carsulae is now a large archaeological area around the small 11th-century church of San Damiano which was built on the site of a Roman building. The site includes the ruins of the forum and the buildings surrounding it, a small four-sided arch and the foundations of two twin temples dating from the Julio-Claudian era. Higher up the hill are the amphitheatre and theatre. Following the track of the Roman road through the meadows one arrives at a triumphal arch, known as Trajan's Arch, beyond which are the ruins of some funerary monuments.

155. The archaeological excavations at Carsulae.

After abandoning Carsulae the inhabitants sought refuge in the nearby *San Gemini* where remains of floor mosaics from a large country villa have been discovered. The fortified town preserves a characteristic medieval appearance. One room of the Palazzo Pretorio is decorated with scenes of knights symbolizing *Good Government* (14th century). Ascending the valley takes us to the abandoned church of San Giovanni de Butris, built in the 15th century by the Order of the Knights of Malta above the arches of a Roman bridge. On the hill above is *Acquasparta*, a well-known spa resort surrounded by medieval walls. It was a feudal possession of the noble Cesi family which numbers among its members Prince Federico Cesi, the founder of the Lincei Academy. The family home, now owned by Perugia University, is home to summer courses in chamber singing devoted to German 'Lied'.

THE VALNERINA

The Valnerina is the valley carved by the Nera river, a tributary of the Tiber, on its route from Visso in the Marches at the foot of the Sibillini Hills as far as the Terni basin. The river flows for most of its length between steep banks – the valley floor has never played an important role in the meagre local economy – crossing one of the most beautiful landscapes in the Apennine range, where man has succeeded in integrating his creations into the natural world without damaging it. Atop every knoll stands a castle and beside every ford or river crossing is a small Romanesque church.

The valley is reached from Terni along the s. 209, or 'Valnerina', constructed at the end of the 19th century to ensure easy transport of the workforce to the factories in the provincial capital. The road, running along the right bank of the river, does not follow the more ancient routes which ran through the hills at right angles to the valley, linking the major Via Flaminia with the Via Salaria. The road along the valley cut off all the hill towns, condemning them to gradual abandon, and limiting the role of Spoleto which previously was the seat of the political administration as capital of the Longobard duchy.

For centuries the people living in the hills and mountains lived within a subsistence economy based on raising livestock and woodcutting, on the reserves of the seasonal workers during the forced winter halt or on activities or expedients which gave rise to a series of nicknames: the 'cerretani', that is the inhabitants of Cerreto, meaning charlatans or tricksters, or the 'norcini', the inhabitants of Norcia, meaning expert sausage-makers.

At the end of the valley is *Arrone*, a hill-top castle in a strategic position on the road linking the duchy of Spoleto with the Kingdom of Naples. The original town, known as La Terra, occupied the summit of a fortified hill where the feudal family of the Arroni had their residence. The Arroni were ardent opponents of Spoleto and of the abbots of Ferentillo. In 1240 the Emperor Frederick II of Swabia stayed here as a guest of the feudatories. The town developed around the ford on the road leading to Rieti. Here stands the Renaissance church of Santa Maria Assunta which preserves in its apse an important cycle of frescoes by Vincenzo Tamagni and Giovanni da Spoleto (1516). On a rocky outcrop on the other side of the Nera is the village of *Montefranco*, founded in 1288 by some

156. The two forts of Ferentillo in a strategic position at the entrance to the valley.

157. The Abbey of San Pietro in Valle standing out amidst the woods of Mount Solenne.

inhabitants of Arrone who had rebelled against the lords of the castle. Sadly the setting has been greatly altered by the thoughtless construction of modern buildings.

The valley, which up to this point is intensively cultivated, narrows abruptly between two ridges of hills at the foot of which lies *Ferentillo*. Access to the town is protected by two triangular castles, Precetto and Matterello, on the slopes on opposite sides of the river. In the crypt of the church of Santo Stefano a Precetto are several mummies. Going on up the gorge we arrive at the abbey of *San Pietro in Valle* rising out of the woods. This ancient Benedictine monastery was founded at the beginning of the 8th century by Faroald II, Duke of Spoleto, and rebuilt in its present form between 996 and 1016 by order of Otto III of Saxony after a Saracen attack. On the walls of the aisleless nave is a very rare cycle of stories from the Old and New Testaments (12th century). The Nera carves a path below Mount Coscerno, and flows alongside Scheggino, a small town where the speciality is excellent Nera trout cooked with black truffles, and the castle of Sant'Anatolia di Narco.

The ancient road followed the left bank of the river, on the opposite side to the s. 209, and passed through the settlements. A short distance away is *Castel San Felice* at the foot of which is the abbey of San Felice di Narco (c. 1190). This building was constructed on the site of a hermitage of the Syrian monks who drained the valley in the 6th century, an event which is symbolically represented in the

158. The Garden of Eden, detail of the cycle of frescoes of the 11th-12th century which adorns the walls of the Church of San Pietro in Valle.

159. Landscape near Sellano.

160. The fertile Norcia valley.

reliefs on the facade. After passing through a narrow point in the valley we reach *Vallo di Nera*, in a position overlooking the exit from the s. 395, the ancient Via Nursina linking Spoleto and Norcia via the Forca di Cerro pass. This road was the main connection between the Valnerina and the Valle Umbra. Vallo di Nera is a hill-top castle with a perfectly preserved layout. The walls of the Franciscan church of Santa Maria (late-13th century) are entirely covered with votive frescoes. The territory of Vallo borders with that of *Borgo*

Cerreto, an important road junction at the confluence with the Vigi torrent; from here the s. 319 leads to the valley of the Menotre in the direction of Foligno and, via the Colfiorito pass, to Camerino in the Marches. Beside the bridge over the Nera is the Franciscan church of San Lorenzo; inside are some recently restored 14th-century frescoes. On the hill above is the castle of Cerreto, the birthplace of the poet Giovanni Pontano (1429-1503) who lived in Naples at the Aragonese court.

From Borgo the mountain road led off towards Cascia, passing through the small town of *Ponte* with an eagle's nest castle built on the site of a pre-Roman settlement; during the early Middle Ages this was the seat of an important Longobard gastaldate, though now it stands lamentably abandoned. The church of Santa Maria was built in 1201.

The confluence with the Corno river is guarded by *Triponzo*, a town long under the control of the Varano family, lords of Camerino. Here the gorge narrows sharply, a problem the Romans overcame by digging a tunnel by hand through which the road passed. The road continued through steep ravines in the direction of Norcia, the road-builders facing great challenges in the harsh setting of the Corno gorge. At some points travellers can see the route of the disused Spoleto-Norcia railway line, a small masterpiece of railway engineering opened in 1926 and dismantled in 1968. The medieval route followed the tops of the hills where numerous abandoned villages can be seen today.

An alternative route is along the s. 209 towards

Visso. At the Chiusita bridge the road abandons the course of the Nera and climbs the valley of the Campiano, between gentler wooded slopes. Atop a hill stands the village of *Preci*, famous in the 16th century for its school of surgery specializing in the treatment of cataracts and gall-stones. In the early Christian era this area was home to a hermitage of Syrian monks who inspired the originator of western monasticism, St Benedict of Norcia.

In the 5th century one of these hermits founded the abbey of Sant'Eustizio which achieved a position of great influence between the 10th and 12th centuries before going into decline after being ceded to a commendatory abbot. The present church dates from 1190, except for the facade, which was completed in 1236. The interior is completely bare following damage wrought by the frequent earthquakes which afflict this corner of the Umbrian-Marchigian Apennines.

The road climbs gently towards the grassy plateau of the Val Castoriana, in a lonely landscape now inhabited only by older residents who are joined during the summer by crowds of emigrants return-

ing for their holidays. During nomadic stock-raising times the valley was an important point of passage on the transhumance routes, and was densely populated. This is testified to by the presence of the rural church of San Salvatore di Campi, beside which the main road runs and the ancient church of Santa Maria, built in an archaeological area mentioned by St Gregory the Great. The medieval church was enlarged to twice its size in the 15th century to accomodate the pilgrims drawn here to venerate a miraculous painting. The offerings made enabled the walls to be covered with paintings, many of which were executed by the Sparapane brothers, members of a local dynasty of painters who worked over a long period in the late 15th century in the area around Norcia.

Once over the Forca di Ancarano pass (1008 m), one unexpectedly enters the fertile basin of Santa Scolastica, framed by the peaks of the Sibillini Hills.

In the middle of the valley is the walled town of *Norcia*. This site has been inhabited since prehistoric times due to its favourable position at the

161

161. *The Church of San Benedetto at Norcia, with the statue dedicated to the saint in the foreground.*

162. *St Benedict, detail of the frescoes of the Sacro Speco di Subiaco, Latium.*

162

chanted by court life he retired to a solitary life at Subiaco, following the example of the Syrian hermits he had met in the Val Castoriana. Here he founded an order of monks following a rule devoted to a balance between contemplative life and manual labour, inspiring religious groups throughout western Christendom. The Benedictine monks have been attributed with the creation of the 'marcite', a complex natural irrigation system on the Santa Scolastica plain. This allows hay to be mown at least 6 times a year, even in the middle of winter, bringing great benefit to an agricultural economy based largely on stock-raising.

Norcia's history has been plagued by the area's seismic activity. The Romanesque revival was swept away by a disastrous earthquake in 1328. Many of the civic buildings were rebuilt after the 1730, 1815 and 1859 earthquakes, and again after the most recent quake in 1979. To resist tremors the houses, including the nobles' mansions, are generally built on two floors, with thick walls reinforced with large scarps.

Fortunately the circle of walls has survived, the gateways being decorated with 14th-century frescoes. The most important historical buildings stand on Piazza San Benedetto: the 19th-century Palazzo Comunale, the 14th-century church of San Benedetto, the cathedral of Santa Maria Argentea (1560) and the Castellina, a massive fortress designed by Vignola (1554-1563) which is to house the local picture gallery (Pinacoteca). If there is time, it is worth visiting the church of *Santa*

border between the Umbrian and Sabine territories. *Nursia* was the furthest north of the Sabine towns, and as such sent volunteers to help the Roman troops during the Second Punic War (205 B.C.). From the Roman period there survive some rooms with floor mosaics in the crypt of San Benedetto, perhaps the remains of a civic basilica but traditionally held to be part of St Benedict's house. Converted to Christianity by the good offices of St Felicianus, the bishop of Foligno, Norcia was the birthplace of St Benedict (480), the founder of monasticism in the West.

The saint was a law student in Rome, but disen-

Cooking

Umbrian cooking has always been popular cooking, simple and genuine, accustomed to tuning daily need to the flow of the seasons, making use of the little or the much that nature offers: milk, eggs, vegetables, pulses, light and fragrant olive oil and excellent pecorino (ewe's milk cheese); woodland produce, mushrooms, asparagus and truffles; poultry, lamb and baby goat at Easter time, geese and ducks at harvest time, fresh pork at Christmas and sausages all year round; wild game when the birds are flying, thrushes and wood-pigeon in October and March; carp and pike from Lake Trasimene, trout from the Nera. A true Umbrian cuisine does not exist because there are as many different cuisines as there are towns, each one distinguished by a traditional dish or special recipes.

The most simple dishes are often the best. 'Torta al Testo', a pizza-bread of flour and water, flavoured with fried pork crackling and pecorino cheese, cooked on a terracotta disc heated over the embers and stuffed with sliced salted meats or with vegetables; 'panzanella', stale bread soaked in water and mixed with tomato, onion and basil; 'bruschetta', toasted home-baked bread with a pinch of salt, plenty of garlic and good olive oil and a generous grating of black truffles; tomatoes stuffed with breadcrumbs, parsley and garlic.

There is no end to the variety. Umbria may not be home to 'lasagne' or 'tortellini', but it is home to some of the most important pasta-manufacturers: Buitoni at Sansepolcro and Perugia, Mignini at Ponte San Giovanni, Spigadoro at Bastia Umbra, Corticella at Foligno, Federici at Amelia. Better still is a steaming plate of home-made 'tagliatelle', flavoured with goose sauce or pork-trimmings and sprinkled with lots of pecorino cheese; 'stringozzi', a sort of spaghetti, with black truffle or cepe mushrooms; or polenta eaten 'sulla spianatora', covered with a sauce made with sausages and pork crackling. The soups include beans with pork trimmings, barley soup and a soup made from the delicious Castelluccio di Norcia lentils which

I. Typical products sold in a Norcia pork-butcher's shop.

II. Jacopo Torriti: The Marriage in Cana. Assisi, Upper Church of San Francesco.

I, II

are grown at an altitude of 1400 m and are therefore pest-free. Main courses include roast pork, and it is no coincidence that the inhabitants of Norcia have given the name 'norcini' to butchers and sausage-makers. In the town's piazzas it is hard to miss the figure of the 'porchettaro' selling roast suckling pig flavoured with wild fennel and plenty of pepper. Specialities of Perugia include roast rump of veal and meatballs with raisins and pinenuts. Between Spoleto and Norcia gastronomes may enjoy mutton chops and excellent roast lamb.

In Todi and Amelia there may be thrush on the spit and wood-pigeon 'alla ghiotta', a sauce made with red wine, the entrails of the bird and herbs, or 'in salmi', with a sauce of shallots, Norcia ham, capers and cloves. On lean days, try carp 'in porchetta', pan-fried eel or fried 'saltarelli' if beside Lake Trasimene, or Nera trout with truffle in the Valnerina.

The sunny hills provide plenty of excellent wine, grouped into six recognized areas of production. The white wine of Orvieto is famous throughout the world. With its straw colour and full flavour it is served as cool as it is when taken out of the cellars dug into the tufa rock.

There are also generous red wines to accompany the meat dishes, such as Rubesco di Torgiano and Sacrantino di Montefalco. The raisin wines include the excellent but hard to find Vernaccia di Cannara.

Umbrians love sweetmeats, but only eat them on certain days of the year, almost as if it were a ritual. On his deathbed St Francis asked to be allowed to eat 'mostaccioli', small biscuits of flour, aniseed and grape must; they are still made in Assisi for the saint's festival. Perugia is famous throughout the world for its Perugina chocolates, but the local's favourite sweetmeat is the 'torcolo di San Costanzo', eaten on 29 January, 'strufoli' and shakes during the carnival, pancakes on St Joseph's Day, sweet maccheroni and 'fave dei Morti' on 2 November, 'pinoccate' and 'stinchetti' at Christmas.

Scolastica in the centre of the plain of the same name. It is entirely covered with frescoes by Jacopo Salimbeni from San Severino and an anonymous follower of Bartolomeo di Tommaso from Foligno (15th century).

A delightful excursion can be made to the Pian Grande di Castelluccio, a closed hollow on a plateau in the Sibillini Hills. Isolated during the winter months by heavy falls of snow, the water disappears with the spring thaw into a shallow hole without leaving any trace. This makes the land particularly fertile, especially suitable for the growing of lentils. During the flowering season the fields are enlivened with a fabulous display of a thousand different colours. From Castelluccio a short walk takes us to the picturesque Lake Pilato on Mount Vettore. According to legend, the body of Pontius Pilate fell into the lake from an ox-drawn cart after he was executed in Rome by Titus Vespasian. On Mount Sibilla one can still see the Grotta delle Fate cave, once inhabited by a Sibyl.

We leave Norcia by the s. 396. At the Serravalle

163. *View of Cascia.*

164. *Crowd of pilgrims in front of the Basilica of Santa Rita at Cascia.*

165. *The extraordinary springtime flowering of the Great Plain of Castelluccio, the vast karst plateau in the Umbro-Marchigian Appenines.*

turning we go up the valley of the Corno towards *Cascia,* a Roman town on the link with Via Salaria. Standing half-way up the slope of the hill, the medieval town has been suffocated by the intensive building which accompanied the large numbers of pilgrims coming to venerate St Rita, who was born in Roccaporena in 1380 and died in 1457. Together with the church of Santa Rita, rebuilt in 1947, one can see the churches of San Francesco (13th century) and Sant'Antonio Abate, the latter decorated by the 'Master of the Terni Dormition' (early 15th century) and Nicola da Siena (1461).

ORVIETO

Perhaps it is only its position in the Tiber valley which links Orvieto to Umbria. The low and gently rolling horizon, the historical roots, the local dialect and the red tufa rock standing out from the stone and the pebbles on the river beds link this land to the common stock of Etruria, to the towns of Barbarano, Blera, Pitigliano and Sovana. For centuries the town was a member of the Papal States and only in 1860 did it become part of Umbria. By cultural tradition, though, Orvieto is tied to Viterbo and Rome, and today it is better connected by rail and motorway to Rome than to the provincial capital Terni or the more distant Perugia. The landscape of this corner of the region stretches from the farmland of the volcanic plateau around Lake Bolsena as far as the valley of the Tiber which, once out of the wild gorges of the Forello, continues its tranquil course towards Latium. Here the river meets the Paglia which rises on Mount Amiata, carves a path through the thick woods of Mount Rufeno and generates the flood plain of Orvieto before flowing into the Chiani. Mainly hilly in nature, the dominant colour is embodied in the reddish tones of the volcanic earth, intensively cultivated with vines and grain.

Whether one arrives from the south via the modern 'Autostrada del Sole', or from the shores of Lake Bolsena along the ancient routes connecting up with Via Cassia, *Orvieto* appears unexpectedly. The cliffs of red rock rise steeply out of the green of the vines stretching off into the distance and the golden background of ripening crops in the valley of the Paglia. The entire town is built on an elliptical tufa outcrop running east-west, tall enough for the town not to need any defensive walls. An important Etruscan town – it was the seat of the *Fanum Voltumnae*, the national shrine of the Etruscan twelve-city league – it was destroyed in 264 B.C. by the Romans and the inhabitants were deported to the shores of Lake Bolsena. Huge necropolises have been discovered dug into the rock. *Volsinii Veteres* remained deserted almost until the 6th century A.D., when the lack of safety offered in the countryside led those who escaped massacre by the Goths to seek shelter behind its natural defences. As a free city during the Middle Ages Orvieto grew considerably in power, expanded as far as the port of Talamello, and was several times the seat of conclaves. Numerous popes chose it as their summer residence, prefer-

ring the coolness of its rocky position refreshed by winds to Rome's torrid climate. The town took up all the available space, pushing outwards to the foot of the outcrop.

Skilled local artisans erected the most important buildings, the outstanding Gothic cathedral, the monastic churches and the public buildings. Orvieto's decline started with the Black Death in 1348 which decimated the population. In 1354 cardinal Albornoz subjected the town to the long-lasting rule of the Church, erecting a fortress here in 1364. Under papal control Orvieto was embellished with outstanding patrician homes designed by the famous architects (Antonio da Sangallo, Michele Sanmichele, Ippolito Scalza) who had been called to oversee the construction of the cathedral.

The road from Bolsena enters the town through the Porta Maggiore gate, beneath the severe eyes of Boniface VIII, whose mania for having statues devoted to him (another image of the Pope is situated at the gate of the fort) resulted in his being subjected to a grotesque post-mortem trial organized by the French king Philip the Fair. The main street climbs between two thick walls dug out of the tufa in Via della Cava and divides the town in two as far as the opposite gate of Porta Soliano. At the Torre del Moro the 'decumanus' crosses the 'cardo', dividing the town into four quarters. Around the edge of the rock runs an encircling road, on which the monastic cloisters and the military buildings stand. The political centre of the town is Piazza della Repubblica with the 13th-century Palazzo Comunale, rebuilt by Scalza, and the church of Sant'Andrea, founded on the site of an Etruscan temple, from which Innocent III announced the Fourth Crusade in 1216. The religious heart beats in the tall spire of the cathedral, founded in 1290 to house a venerated holy relic. Here we see the exceptional meeting between the enormous dimensions of a Gothic bulk and the loving detail of ornamental decoration, in that "local but exquisite medieval crucible blending enamels, glass and mosaics, *sculptilia et pictilia*", as Roberto Longhi writes, summing up the character of Orvieto's design. Walking through the medieval quarters of this beautiful town, in a maze of tangled lanes where the sign of an inn entices the visitor to sip a glass of the fragrant local wine beneath the shade of a pergola, we slip past the Palazzo Papale built by Martin IV (1281-84) and Palazzo Soliano commissioned

166. *The Orvietan countryside.*

167

167. *View of Orvieto with the spires of the Cathedral.*

168, 169. *The Church of*
Sant'Andrea with its bell-
tower and one of the town
quarters of Orvieto.

168

169

170

by Boniface VIII (1297-1304), now housing the Museo Capitolare. The many-coloured Piazza del Mercato is dominated by the Gothic Palazzo del Capitano del Popolo (12th-13th century). A little lower down is to be found what remains of the church of San Domenico, inside which is a beautiful tomb carved by the Florentine sculptor Arnolfo di Cambio (c. 1283). At the edge of the hill stands the Romanesque church of San Giovenale (1004), its walls entirely covered with frescoes. One can descend into the heart of the rock via the slippery steps of the San Patrizio well, dug to a design by Sangallo at the time of the sack of Rome in 1527. Further down are the Etruscan tombs in the *Crocifisso del Tufo* necropolis (7th-3rd century B.C.), the tombs flanking the burial walkways to create a sort of city of the dead.

Near Orvieto are some rural villages grown up around antique feudal castles (Castel Viscardo, Castello Rubello, Allerona). A rarer sight, due to the abandonment of the countryside by sharecroppers, are the settlements along the s. 71, an

170. *The Church of San Giovanni at Orvieto.*

171. *The Church of San Giovenale at Orvieto.*

172. *A characteristic medieval lane in Orvieto.*

173. *The Cathedral of Orvieto, dedicated to Our Lady of the Assumption, one of the most important monuments in the region.*

important road between Via Cassia and the Casentino, ascending the valley of the Chiani beside Mount Peglia (Ficulle, Parrano) in an area rich with Mediterranean maquis vegetation, with natural canyons, mineral water springs and prehistoric caves. At Fabro the valley widens, opening up into the Valdichiana. The Tuscan side is bounded by the bulk of the Cetona, a fine green-clad hill with a pretty medieval village. Towards Umbria runs a huge range of hills between Lake Trasimene and the valley of the Nestore.

1

172

173

The Miracle of the Duomo

In the summer of 1263 Pope Urban IV was staying in Orvieto with his court. A Bohemian priest who doubted the presence of the body of Christ in the host, while celebrating mass in the church of Santa Cristina in Bolsena saw some drops of blood emerge from the host and stain the altar and corporal. As soon as he heard of the miracle, Urban sent Bishop Giacomo to Bolsena to take the holy cloth and awaited his arrival at the foot of Orvieto's rock, before accompanying the relic in a procession into the old cathedral. Orvieto's spiritual life was at that time troubled by the Patarine heresy, and on 11 August 1264 the pope combated it with the proclamation of the dogma of the Corpus Domini. Thomas Aquinas, at that time a teacher of philosophy at the Dominican convent in the town, was charged with composing a solemn hymn. Finally, on 11 November 1290, in the presence of Nicholas IV, Bishop Francesco Monaldeschi laid the first stone of the new cathedral, almost as a majestic reliquary turned towards Bolsena.

In its colossal dimensions, which cannot be appreciated when forced to look at it from near at hand as the small space bids, the building is inspired by the model of contemporary French cathedrals, though adapted to demands and to local precedents. The overseer of the building work from 1290 to 1300 was Fra Bevignate from Perugia, who had also worked on the Fontana Maggiore in Perugia together with Nicola Pisano. Bevignate took full advantage of local motifs present in the architecture of the mendicant orders, such as the use of the vault limited to the area of the presbytery and the trussed roof of the nave and aisles. Bas-reliefs on facades had already appeared in Spoleto's Romanesque architecture, but here they are turned to such a realistic narrative effect that they seem to be illustrated tapestries hung from the pillars.

In 1308 Lorenzo Maitani was called to Orvieto from Siena to solve some practical problems in the apse, and it was under his direction that the reliefs of the facade, carved by that

I

II

I, II. Detail of the facade of the Cathedral with the symbols of the Evangelists and one of the 14th-century bas-reliefs representing the Last Judgement.

V. Luca Signorelli: detail of The Damned, one of the frescoes which decorate the Chapel of San Brizio.

feverish group of sculptors and stone-cutters, smiths and carpenters, painters and glaziers which can be traced through the archive documents, were mounted.

The tall facade is designed like an open book in honour of the Virgin Mary, to whom the cathedral is dedicated. At the base of the three pillars there are stories from Genesis, the geneaology of Christ and stories of the Evangelists supporting images in bronze of the Evangelists. The mosaics depict Mary's life on earth, culminating in the Assumption and the Coronation. The decoration of the interior was extensively altered at the end of the 16th century when the altars were remade to adapt them to the rules pronounced by the Council of Trent and was largely lost in the purist restorations carried out at the end of the 19th century which stripped the walls of the nave and heavily repainted the frescoes in the chapel of the Corporale and the tribune in the apse. Mary's centrality as symbol of the Church reappears in the large stained-glass window by Giovanni di Bonino (1334) and in the apsidal tribune. The main altars

in the transept are dedicated to the Miracle of Bolsena (the cloth is preserved in a precious reliquary executed by the Sienese goldsmith Ugolino di Vieri) and to the stories of the Last Judgement in the chapel of San Brizio, decorated with celebrated frescoes by Luca Signorelli (1500).

III, IV

III. Gentile da Fabriano: detail of the Madonna and Child, a fresco in the left aisle of the Cathedral.

IV. The Reliquario del Corporale, executed by Ugolino di Vieri in the 14th century.

V

174

175

174, 175. The Palazzo del Popolo and the Pozzo di San Patrizio, one of the attractions of Orvieto.

176

176. The Etruscan necropolis of Crocifisso del Tufo in the immediate surroundings of Orvieto.

177. Attic-style Etruscan pottery from the Museo Claudio Faina in Orvieto.

177

INDEX OF ILLUSTRATIONS